Coming from the Light

"All too soon it was time for us to part one another's company. I knew I was in another world, another dimension, a dream. I wanted something tangible to hold on to so I would remember. So I asked her for her name. She whispered in a melodic sound of song, 'Trisna.' Then she vanished. . . ."

—from "Irisna's Song"

". . . after that day, Jennica never talked about or to Grandma Liz. Two weeks later, while helping me with the dishes, she looked out the window and started waving:

" 'Why are you waving?' I asked.

" 'I'm saying goodbye to Jesus. He's in the castle,' she responded.

" 'What castle?'

" 'The one I lived in before I came to live with you. . . .' "

—from "The Castle Where Jesus Lived"

"One of my most cherished possessions is a picture of our daughter, Cherilee, with blond, curly, bouncy hair and shining, laughing, blue-green eyes; the same little girl I saw with my friend Lee as his spirit was leaving the earth and her spirit was preparing to come down. . . ."

—from "When Spirits Meet"

COMING FROM THE LIGHT

LIGHT

Spiritual Accounts of Life Before Life

SARAH HINZE

POCKET BOOKS
New York   London   Toronto   Sydney   Tokyo   Singapore

POCKET BOOKS, a division of Simon & Schuster Inc.
1230 Avenue of the Americas, New York, NY 10020

Copyright © 1994, 1997 by Sarah Hinze

Published by arrangement with Cedar Fort Incorporated

All rights reserved, including the right to reproduce this book or portions thereof in any form whatsoever. For information address Cedar Fort Incorporated, c/o Onjinjinkta Productions, P.O. Box 66119, Seattle, WA 98166

ISBN: 0-671-00159-0

First Pocket Books trade paperback printing January 1997

10 9 8 7 6 5 4 3 2 1

POCKET and colophon are registered trademarks of Simon & Schuster Inc.

Cover design by Tom McKeveny
Cover photo by John Morrison/Photonica

Printed in the U.S.A.

In Memory Of

Joyce Alger Straley, whose constant prayers were for this book and who died June 29, 1991. Her loving presence has been felt in the progress of this work and especially in its completion.

Dedication

Before I formed thee in the belly I knew thee;
and before thou camest forth out of the womb I sanctified thee. . . .
—Jeremiah 1:5

It is to the preborn spirits in the kingdom on high who await birth,
to the multitudes of royal children preparing to come down,
to the reawakening of the royal child within each of us,
that I dedicate this work.

Acknowledgments

To the source of the Light, even Jesus Christ, for His divine inspiration.

To countless individuals who have shared a story, handed me a meaningful quotation, or narrated so humbly their experiences of life before life, I give my heartfelt gratitude. You have shared a portion of yourselves that we may know more about the Light and the source of our own coming.

A special thanks to Dr. Eugene Seaich for his friendship and profound scholarship of the ancient texts, which he has shared with extraordinary generosity.

To Debbie Cross for her inspiration and enduring friendship.

To my husband, Brent, for his love, sacrifices, and dedicated editorial assistance. His tender respect and insight into this material has been a major factor in its completeness.

To our children, Krista, Laura, Rodney, Tadd,

Sarah, Matthew, Samuel, Rachel, and Anna, who taught us about the Light, even as they came into our home.

To our son-in-law, Randy, and our grandchildren, Wayne Scott and Jessica Elaine, for the love they so willingly share.

To our foster children, and all of our friends and loved ones who have been so supportive of me during an intense and often refining journey of compiling this book, I express my deepest thanks for their love, encouragement, and prayers.

To my parents for their encouragement that I continually strive for my highest dreams. My father passed away in November 1995:

"We miss you, Dad, but we know that you are still nearby from time to time, checking in on us."
"Mom, I love you with all my heart and soul. Continue in the courage to carry on."

My heartfelt thanks to my agent, Tom Eadie, and Onjinjinkta Productions for your conviction to assist me in taking this message to the world. Your aid at a difficult time was a direct answer to my prayers. God's speed as you move forward with your mission.

My deepest gratitude to Paul Perry, Dr. Elisabeth Kübler-Ross, Dr. Kenneth Ring, and especially Betty J.

ACKNOWLEDGMENTS

Eadie. Your support and encouragement are a most remarkable gift.

And finally, thanks to Simon and Schuster and to editors Claire Zion, Danielle Dayen, Dan Slater, and Tom Spain, who provided expert advice while giving me the freedom to fill my mission.

xi

Foreword

by Paul Perry

Coauthor of *Closer to the Light,*
Transformed by the Light,
and *Saved by the Light*

For almost ten years now I have been involved in a field of psychological research known as near-death studies. This is an exciting field of study for a number of reasons, not the least of which is the fact that it is fraught with controversy.

The main basis of research in this field is case studies of people who have almost died. At the moment of personal extinction, these people have what they often describe as being the most glorious experiences of their whole life. They have such phenomena as leaving their body, zooming up a tunnel of light, seeing marvelous beings of light, including dead relatives, having a life review, seeing a sort of master-being of light that many describe as God, and then having the sensation of returning to their bodies.

Virtually all of these people are transformed by their experiences. They become kinder, have a greater zest for life, and have even been known to pick up psychic abilities.

Medical doctors used to deny that near-death experiences take place. They said that the patient was merely having a dream or that these marvelous events were just a vivid form of wish fulfillment. Sometimes they even declared the patient insane.

Luckily those days are past. Now, thanks to the field of near-death studies, modern medicine recognizes the existence of these experiences. Many doctors now accept as fact that these experiences happen to their patients.

But near-death experiences are the wellspring for other types of controversy. Are they proof of life after death, or just a good dream? Are they proof that the spirit can leave the body, or is the out-of-body phenomenon just a psychological response known as disassociation?

There are many questions, and frankly no one knows the true answer to them, but we continue to collect stories and the research goes on.

I thought I had heard every question there was to ask about the near-death experience. Then I got a call one day from Sarah Hinze. She asked me something I had never even considered: "Do the people you gather case studies from often see spirits waiting to be born?"

"No," was my immediate answer, but I promised that I would search my case studies just to make sure. In doing that I was surprised to find a number of people who had witnessed the very thing she was talking about.

In one such case, an oil worker in Texas told me about his near-death experience, which took place when he was fifteen. He lived on the Gulf Coast of that state and spent most of his free time playing along the beach and swamplands near his hometown.

One day, as he was wading through the swamp, he stepped into a deep pool and was knocked unconscious when he struck his head on a rock. A friend who was with him ran for help, which eventually arrived or I would never have heard this story. He told me what happened as he was underwater:

I do remember hitting that rock and then there was nothing. The next thing I knew I was zooming up a tunnel that was bright and colorful, like a tube full of carnival lights. At the end of the tunnel was a place that just looked like heaven. There were hills and trees, but they weren't like the trees we have here; they were bright and all lighted up.

I met a man there who was real big. I couldn't see his face because he glowed so beautifully, but from his voice I could tell that he was real nice.

He told me that I would be going back. I was glad about that, but I didn't go back right away. I walked around in these hills. It was like being on the moon.

I could sort of jump and cover about fifty yards with each step. I took a few steps like this, and I bounded right into a bunch of kids like myself.

The man was with me. He told me to enjoy myself, that I would be going back before these people were.

"What do you mean?" I asked.

"These are people who haven't been to earth yet," he said.

This man wasn't sure how to interpret this message. Did that mean they were going to be reincarnated? Did it mean that they were "new" spirits just waiting for their turn on earth? Now, forty years after falling into that pond and having a near-death experience, he was still wondering just who those other kids were that he saw in that spiritual realm.

Other case studies that I have gathered mirror the stories that you will read in this book. One woman told of nearly dying and going to a "spiritual place" where she saw her infant daughter who had died several years earlier. With her child were many other children of the same age. This woman told me that she was sure these were "people waiting to be born."

Others like her have made similar observations. A seven-year-old girl named Jamie, who was one of the cases featured in *Transformed by the Light*, which I wrote with Dr. Melvin Morse, had a near-death experience the day she was declared dead by medical doctors. She felt her consciousness leave her body, and she watched as doctors and nurses stood around her bed.

"Suddenly everything went all dark and I was scared," she said. "I floated up and I was in heaven. There was a huge rainbow. There were people there, you know, waiting to be born."

One of the most detailed near-death experiences I have ever heard came from Dannion Brinkley of South Carolina, who had the misfortune of being struck by lightning while on the telephone. As paramedics tried to start his heart, he had one of these spiritual adventures that took him to a "crystal city," where he encountered many beings of light. Some of these beings talked to him about the courage it takes to leave the spirit world and be reborn unto a mortal existence.

"Humans are powerful spiritual beings," he said. The implication was that we as humans are on a sort of missionary trip to make God's will happen.

The belief in premortal existence is nothing new. The ancient Greeks, for instance, spoke of the immortality of the spirit and of a premortal state for man. Plato, responding to Socrates in the *Phaedo*, said:

> *Your favorite doctrine, Socrates, that knowledge is simply recollection, if true, also necessarily implies a previous time in which we have learned that which we now recollect. But this would be impossible unless our soul has been in some place before existing in the form*

of man; here then is another proof of the soul's immortality.

There is considerable evidence to suggest that belief in premortal existence was openly discussed in the early Christian Church. St. Augustine taught of man's premortal state, writing, "When we reason it is the mind that reasons. . . . For what is thought is eternal, and nothing pertaining to the body is thus eternal. . . . Therefore the human mind always lives." Perhaps no Christian scholar spoke more extensively of premortal existence than Origen of Alexandria. He stirred up controversy in the third-century church with his belief that some sort of judgment had already taken place before we came to earth. This judgment was based on work done in a premortal state.

As Origen wrote, "We believe that he was even then chosen by God because of merits acquired before this life."

Origen's teachings were attacked by critics who considered these thoughts as being too Greek. In A.D. 543, the Roman emperor Justinian convinced the pope to convene a council to reject the teachings of Origen. Since then, the concept of premortal existence has faded. Now, most mainstream religions either speak out against it or have no feelings one way or the other.

Still, people continue to have visions of those waiting to be born, regardless of official church doctrine. It is just such visions that make up the pages of this book.

Frankly, I don't know just what to make of these case studies that have been compiled by Sarah Hinze. Are they proof of premortal existence? Are they proof of anything but the human brain's capacity to keep its owner happy with a fantasy that we are indeed immortal? I just don't know. I do know, however, that by reading such case studies a person with an inquiring mind has more information on which to base his or her personal beliefs.

Anyway you cut it, the message contained in these case studies is intriguing, as is the poetry of what they have to say. For instance, I like to think that the entire debate over premortal existence comes down to these two sentences that were taken from Betty Eadie's book. "If you could see yourself before you were born, you would be amazed at your intelligence and glory," she wrote in *Embraced by the Light*. "Birth," as Wordsworth intimated, "is but a sleep and a forgetting."

What a fine notion that is.

Contents

CONTENTS

Before my Tongue or Cheeks were
To me shewn,
Before I knew my Hands were
Mine,
Or that my Sinews did my
Members joyn,
When neither Nostril, Foot, or
Ear,
As yet was seen or felt, or did
Appear;
I was within
A House I knew not, newly
Clothed with Skin.

Then was my Soul my only All to
Me.
A Living Endless Eye,
Just bounded with the Skie
Whose Power, whose Act, whose
Essence was to see.
I was an inward Sphere of Light,
Or an Interminable Orb of Sight,
An Endless and a Living Day,
A vital Sun that round about did
Ray
All Life, all Sence,
A Naked Simple Pure Intelligence.

—THOMAS TRAHERNE
"The Perspective"

The Lord told the Apostles, "They will ask you where you are going." And He told them to answer, "To the place from which I came. I return to that place."

When they ask you who you are, say, "I am a son and I come from the Father."

And when they ask you what sort of son and from what father, answer, "From the preexistent Father and I am a son of the Preexistence."

—The Apocryphon of James

I Knew My Children Before Birth

My interest in "life before life" is very personal. Before each of our nine children was born, I sensed that he or she was preparing to come to earth. I prayed for the safe arrival of each of these special spirits. On several occasions I had come to know that these souls wanted to join our family. As my spirituality and respect for motherhood grew, I received the gift of increasing visits from my preborn through the veil. I could feel that each child had a unique personality and that it was their time to come to earth with a personal mission only they could fill. I believe this is true for all of us.

As I share portions of my personal story, I do not want you to think these very private and special events were a common occurrence for me. Remember, these hallowed experiences are now condensed for the telling. They actually unfolded over a period of several years, and I had to endure dry periods by faith alone. I have prayerfully determined it is time to share what I know—that our eternal spirit is the true self, the self that lives before, during and after earth life.

With my fifth pregnancy I sorrowed greatly upon losing the baby to miscarriage. I had felt this gentle female presence with me before she was even conceived. During the three months her tiny earth body grew within me, her spirit self would occasionally enter my dreams and share with me her love. After the miscarriage I feared that I had lost her forever.

Then God comforted me.

Within two months I was shown in a dream that I had only lost this girl child temporarily . . . that she would have a second chance for birth through me. I saw her mature spirit. I marveled at her radiance. Her shoulder-length brown hair was pulled back behind her head, and her large brown eyes were inquisitive. She was apprehensive about her sojourn on earth and reluctant to leave behind the loving environment and special friends of the premortal realm. However, in this dream she committed to come to earth . . . she called me "Mother."

Several months later in dream-vision I was shown a hospital room. I saw every detail—the narrowness of the room, the window, the bed, the television. I saw the door open and a nurse walk in with a little bundle. I rejoiced when she placed a beautiful baby girl in my arms.

As I awakened from the dream, I sensed a divine, loving, male presence standing in the doorway to my bedroom. In a distinct voice, he decreed of the female infant I had just seen in my dream, "Her name is Sarah. Her name is Sarah."

Not many days after this miraculous experience I conceived again. During the critical third month of pregnancy I threatened to miscarry a second time. As the pain and hemorrhaging increased, I was frightened. I fell to the floor in total humility. I prayed, desperately pleading to God with all the power of my being, "Please help me."

Eyes closed, a vision unfolded in my mind. I saw my spirit self departing our heavenly home. The celestial firmament was enveloped in brilliant light, an eternal burning of holy flames that did not consume. It was the place where God dwells. Separating from our Heavenly Father is heart wrenching. I felt an intense sadness as I moved down through space. I was leaving a place where I had been safe, loved unconditionally for eons of time. But I knew it was time to embark on my mission to mortality.

As I continued traveling down through the stars, the pace accelerated. Then I saw it, the earth far, far below—forbidding, distant, cold. A stark contrast from heaven. I'd been taught in my premortal life that earth was a long way from our heavenly abode. But when I actually experienced the journey to earth, I was awed by the cosmic distance.

I felt the chill of the approaching remote and dreary world. Fear and loneliness filled my being as the abyss widened from the nurturing, peaceful and loving environment of my celestial childhood. Comfort appeared in a presence, a strengthening escort who emerged by my side. He was male. Telepathically I conveyed to my escort, "I did not realize that the earth was *so* far away from our heavenly home."

"Indeed, it is a great distance," he acknowledged.

As the vision faded, a message of hope entered my mind: "You came to the earth to be tested and tried, but you shall overcome the trial of this threatened miscarriage."

Reawakening to my immediate surroundings, I found myself in prostrate humility, flat on the floor. I sensed a Being of power enter the room. I felt compelled to rise. I cannot explain how, but I knew it was Jesus Christ. I was totally immersed in His love. I begged Him to heal my body for the sake of the child within me. In answer, He conveyed these words to my mind:

"I am the Great Physician. I will heal your body, and this baby will be born whole and well, for I have so decreed it." The promise delivered, His presence gently withdrew. I rested upon the bed, enveloped in a peaceful, healing power. Soon, the pain and hemorrhaging stopped entirely. I was whole. And, above all, my baby was safe!

Months later, when the time for birthing arrived, my husband and I traveled to the hospital. It was a cold, dark night. As the car cut through the relentless rain, I closed my eyes to the soothing rhythm of the windshield wipers. In my mind I saw a beautiful girl with brown hair and brown eyes. She was saying good-bye to many people, all dressed in white in the heavenly realm. I was eager to receive my promised namesake, little Sarah, but I could sense that she was apprehensive about leaving the unconditional love of her celestial home. I feared that she might withdraw from earth life again. I prayed for the safe arrival of our sweet girl child.

When I opened my eyes, we were nearing the hospital. I checked in and was wheelchaired to my room. The labor went well. I was nearly ready to move to the delivery room when the doctor stepped out momentarily. With my husband comforting me as best he could, I approached those final few minutes before birth when things get most challenging. I again closed my eyes and prayed silently. With my spiritual eyes, I saw

7

the outline of a personage dressed in white, standing at the foot of the bed.

"I have personally escorted this child to mortality," he announced.

I was much relieved by this assurance that little Sarah would not "back out" again—that her apprehension for earth life was overcome by the aid of a divine escort. Shortly thereafter, our precious daughter was born.

Soon a nurse came in and said, "Every room on the maternity floor is full. We must move you down to an area we seldom use on the second floor." I was gurneyed through long corridors and down elevators to an isolated little room. As they propped me up in my bed, mental images from a year earlier flooded my mind. I had seen this exact room in dream-vision, along with the events that followed.

The door opened and a nurse walked in with a little bundle. She placed the gift in my arms. As I looked deeply into the eyes of my beautiful baby girl, it was as if I heard the proclaiming voice echo from the past, "Her name is Sarah. Her name is Sarah." At last I held my namesake—Sarah Rebekah—the sweet baby of my dream, whose earthly body had miscarried on the first try, now returned to earth as promised, our mortal child.

When Sarah Rebekah, now known as Becky, was seven months old, we observed the very sweet nature in this child. Upon awakening from a nap, she would coo and sing and try to talk in an adorable manner. We kidded among our family, which included several foster daughters at the time, that Becky must be "talking with the angels." We came to know that this statement was more fact than fiction.

One afternoon Becky announced with melodic cooing that she had awakened from her nap. I approached her room, but momentarily paused. I felt an unusual sensation, and I knew that I was crossing onto holy ground. I hesitated to even touch the doorknob for fear I would disturb the sacred feeling. At last I felt I could proceed. I reverently opened the door, peering in cautiously. The hallowed feeling was coming from a male presence hovering angel-like over Becky's crib. I cannot say that I saw him with my natural eyes, but rather with some inner knowledge greater than sight. Little Becky was cooing with great joy as we both soaked in the pure love radiating from the spiritual visitor.

Absorbed in this heavenly scene, I heard with my spiritual ears a male voice flow from the presence in the room, "Tell Mother I need to come now."

All the while, Becky was looking intently upward, kicking her little feet, her face glowing radiantly. She was speaking what to me was child's babble, but I sensed this was her effort to communicate with her brother in her former celestial tongue, through a cumbersome earthly body to which she was not yet accustomed. (Infant crying is often the simple frustration of an eternal

9

spirit striving to learn to control an earthly body. The spirit-self moves much more freely than the physical self. Let us be patient with the little ones as they learn earth life.)

By this time I was overcome with tears of the Spirit. We were honored by a prebirth visitation from Becky's future brother, who was announcing it was his time to come to earth. The sacred experience faded as my future son concluded his mission and departed. I have come to understand that the unborn often visit their future families and homes. (The imaginary friends of small children may not be fictitious. Some "friends" may be imaginary only to us adults.)

Our future son departed, but within a month he again crossed the veil to impress upon me the time had arrived for his conception. I shared this message from the celestial timetable with my husband, and became pregnant that very night.

Near the end of the first trimester of pregnancy, I was visited a third time by our future son's spirit. He announced, "My name is Matthew." Each time that I had been privileged to be in the presence of my pre-born, Matthew, I sensed his predominant personality traits—love and gentleness.

Months later I was heavy with child. Following the custom of gathering our children daily for family prayer, one day we formed a kneeling circle in the living room. After prayer, our then ten-year-old daughter, Laura, had tears in her eyes and wonderment on her face. I quote from Laura, now age twenty-four:

> *During the prayer I opened my eyes and looked up. I saw the spirit of a man about six feet two inches tall with blond hair and smooth olive skin. His spirit was pure and loving. He was dressed in white attire with a V neck. He had a broad chest and shoulders. He had bare feet and bare forearms. His hands were on the shoulders of my kneeling father. As I gazed at him, I knew I had known and loved him forever. He was someone that I loved more than life itself. He was my brother Matthew.*

Matthew is now fourteen. He is developing as Laura saw him in her vision years ago. Today, in spite of the ten years difference in their earth ages (we don't know who is oldest eternally), Laura and Matthew are deeply bonded. They do many things together, such as water-skiing and leaping off of thirty-foot cliffs into the Rio Salado during tubing season. They have similar personality traits. They are both daring, but tenderhearted, and quick to lend a helping hand when a job needs doing. Laura says of Matthew, "I know he's going to be a handsome man because I have seen his adult spirit."

A week before Matthew was born, I was sitting in my rocking chair alone late at night, feeling tired and weary with my pregnancy. (You know how it is when you are too tired to go to bed.) I meditated upon the loving presence I had felt several times from Matthew's unborn spirit. Suddenly my preborn son Matthew appeared, standing before me dressed in white, tall and well-formed. I saw his dusty blond hair and handsome rugged features. He thanked me for the sacrifices of pregnancy I was undergoing, nurturing his body within me so he could come to earth and begin his mortal mission. He informed me he would be born within a few days. Then he was gone. This precious son was born a week later, bringing a spirit of heavenly unconditional love to our family.

I am not alone in a belief that every person comes to earth from heaven. The following pages contain selections from over one hundred fifty stories I have collected on our divine origin . . . on "Coming from the Light."

—SARAH HINZE

Happy those early days when I
Shined in my angel-infancy!
Before I understood this place
Appointed for my second race,
Or taught my soul to fancy aught
But a white celestial thought;
When yet I had not walked above
A mile or two from my first love,
And looking back at that short space,
Could see a glimpse of his bright face.

—HENRY VAUGHN
"The Retreat"

Coming from the Light

I AM A NAVAJO NATIVE AMERICAN. I GREW UP ON THE reservation in Tohatchi, New Mexico. The turning point in my life came when I was sixteen years old—I said my first sincere prayer. It is a cherished moment I keep stored in my heart. I remember the desperate feeling of being very lonely as I knelt on the floor next to my nephew's crib, the only private place I could find in our home at the time. At first, I could smell the tortillas my mother was making for dinner. But as I prayed, I soon lost track of earthly surroundings and my soul was consumed by a profound sense of heavenly love and comfort. The divine warmth I discovered in prayer that special day I have since felt over and over as the years have come and gone.

While kneeling, I poured out my desires for a marriage blessed by God. Suddenly I saw an arm pointing to one side. I looked in that direction and a voice said, "Here is your husband." The man I saw was not Native American.

Several years before meeting the "husband" of my vision, my father came to breakfast one morning and told the family of a dream he'd had in which he was holding a baby girl in his arms—the granddaughter he had wanted for years. At the time he had only grandsons. He announced this granddaughter was half white. Because I had told them of my prayer-vision, all eyes fell on me. Years later, my father's dream would come true when he held his first granddaughter (my first daughter) in his arms with the greatest smile, saying, "This is her, the little girl of my dream so long ago. Look at her. She looks exactly the same."

In time, I met the "husband" I had seen during that special experience of my first sincere prayer. When I saw him, I could not deny my inner, burning feeling of "coming home." We fell in love and eventually married on a beautiful summer morning.

Our marriage has been blessed by God and blessed

with children. Each child has brought us joy and moments to treasure. Here is one of those treasures:

It was a chilly autumn morning. As I knelt to say my prayers, something wondrous happened. I felt someone was behind me. I turned around and found myself at the end of a great hall. At the other end of this hall was a door, halfway open, with light shining from behind it. As the door opened wider, not only could I see the brightness of this heavenly light, I could feel it. From the heavenly light I could hear quiet voices and soft footsteps coming toward me. . . .

She was beautiful. Her hair fell naturally around her shoulders. She walked with a young man. They held hands while they talked happily. They stopped near me and embraced. She told him it was time for her to go—to earth—that there she would soon see him again. They held hands until their separating paths pulled them apart—she to be born on earth and he to remain in heaven a short while longer.

As she walked toward me, she began to fade from my vision. But I could still feel her near me—like a soft gentle breeze. I knew she was our daughter. I knew I was going to give birth to a beautiful girl. I turned my head and found myself still kneeling in prayer.

I was so excited to have been shown I would bear a daughter that I began to wear maternity clothes that very day . . . and did so every day for the next nine months. When my husband arrived home that evening he was puzzled and said, "Why are you wearing *those* clothes?"

I joyfully replied I was pregnant, that I knew we would have a daughter and had already picked out her name. So certain was I of my pregnancy that I did not bother going to the doctor to verify it. I simply knew! My husband believed and rejoiced with me.

Our daughter was born nine months later, with her father jumping for joy. "It's a girl, it's a girl!"

I knew it all along.

My father calls our daughter his "dream girl." To me, she looks the same and smiles the same as she did the moment I first saw her in my vision, coming through the heavenly light with all the joy behind it. I know that the mortal body and eternal soul of this daughter came together at the moment of conception.

I thank God for this sacred knowledge.

WANDA O.

Cuddle your soft bundle and tuck your little ones close to your heart, embrace your husband tenderly and rest assured there is no more real spiritual path than motherhood. You are a highly privileged child of God to have been given such a blessing.

—QAHIRA QALBI

An Angel in Overalls

AT THE TIME, TOM AND I HAD FIVE CHILDREN, RANGing from nine to two and a half. Our oldest was a girl, followed by four little boys. Tom was in the construction business. The recession was hitting us pretty hard and money was very tight. The only kind of birth control that seemed to work for us was the IUD. Knowing how unsuccessful most birth control was for us, Tom came to me and asked how I felt about doing some permanent birth control. All the reasons he gave were valid and deserved consideration.

I decided that I would make it a matter of prayer. I wanted to be sure that there were no more children that needed to come to our family.

Sometime later, while I was cleaning the kitchen, I noticed a little toddler with curly hair. She was dressed in a white T-shirt and blue overalls. At first I thought it was one of my little boys getting up from his nap. So I stopped and watched. The little personage peeked around the corner and then toddled into the family room, squatted on the floor, and played for about five minutes. Then he was gone.

I sat and thought about what I had seen. I had seen a spirit. But I was not scared. I felt very peaceful.

The very next day, about the same time, I was in the kitchen again. My husband had the two little boys and the older children were at school. Again, I saw the same little child with curls all over its head, dressed in a white T-shirt and blue overalls. I saw the child peep around the corner, toddle into the family room, play on the floor for about five minutes, and disappear.

At that point, I knew without a doubt that this little child came to remind me that he was waiting to come to our family. I knew that I could not deny what I had experienced. I had to tell Tom. But I could not figure out how to tell him. We had never experienced anything like this.

About three days later we went out to dinner and I tried to tell Tom what happened. I spent the first five minutes trying to tell him that I really wasn't crazy. He spent the next five asking me to quickly tell him what it was I wanted to say. I told him what had happened and explained to him that I thought another child was waiting to come to our family and I believed that it was probably another boy because of the way the personage was dressed. Tom believed me and said that we could have the baby, but we would have to wait until later in the year.

A couple of weeks later, on a Friday, I was cramping a lot and I felt that I needed to get to a doctor that same day. I talked to Tom, and he said that I should have the IUD removed. I knew that it had to be that day. I called my doctor and he was out of town. I called eight other doctors and finally found one that could see me that day. He removed the IUD and didn't see any infection, but gave me a prescription for tetracycline just in case. For some reason I didn't understand at the time, I could not bring myself to get it filled.

During the next several weeks I started to have symptoms of being pregnant. I went to my doctor and found that I was indeed expecting. I told him when I had had the IUD removed. He told me that on that date I was already about ten days pregnant and that I should have had a spontaneous abortion as a result of having the IUD removed. He told me that this baby must really need to come to our family.

In November of 1982 the baby did come. Her dad ended up delivering her in the hallway of the hospital.

By the time she was eighteen months old, she had curls all over her head. And when she was dressed in a white T-shirt and blue overalls, I recognized her as the toddler that visited me twice to let me know that she needed to come to our family.

MINDY R.

With the soul of Adam the souls of all the generations of man were created. They are stored up in a promptuary, in the seventh of the heavens, whence they are drawn as they are needed for human body after human body.

—B. Chagiga 2B
Ancient Text

A Face in the Clouds

I LIVE NEAR THE TOWN OF GERALDTON, AUSTRALIA, about four hours from Perth. To our north is the land of the Aborigines, the Australian outback.

I was fortunate to have a few days off. My workmates and I had planned a weekend on Tasmania, an island south of Australia. It was a long way to travel from our home on the coast of western Australia for just a weekend. But because of my employment with Ansett Airline Company, the tickets were cheap enough and there were seats available on the flights we needed. My wife was eight months pregnant with our fifth child, but she agreed to my short trip.

Following our flight, we drove a lot and slept little.

We did as many touristy things as possible, given the little amount of time we had.

But the most striking event happened as we were just north of Bicheno on the east coast of the island of Tasmania heading north. As we came around a slight bend, there was a small creek where the road dipped down to a crossing. There were thick trees in the creek bed. My eyes were drawn suddenly to the sky above the trees, and a young child's face appeared in the clouds. At that moment, I knew that there was a sixth child waiting to come to our family.

I returned home and not long after the birth of our fifth child, my wife became pregnant again. Prior to my sacred experience, we had thought we would have no more than five children. Now we have six, and the youngest is a boy.

—DES HILL

They are not of the world,
even as I am not of the world.

—JOHN 17:16

My Unborn Son

ONE EVENING, YEARS AGO, MY WIFE AND I SAT ALONE together in the playroom of our house. The children were all asleep in their beds, and we were waiting for the birth of a new little baby. My wife, big with child, was sitting by the table. We were talking softly together, believing that the baby would arrive that night. The lights were low, and there was a feeling of love for each other and for the baby that was to come. I remember looking at my wife—she was rocking quietly, her eyes closed, her pale white hands spread across her full waist. The sweet feeling in the room grew and persisted. It was very powerful. I said to her, "Do you feel this all around us?" and she replied, "Yes." It was lovely being with her there, then. It was a sweet closeness, a unity I can hardly describe.

"Can you tell?" I said. "We will have a son."

"I know," she replied. "It will be a boy."

And then for me the veil parted, and I saw our son, standing, waiting, a few feet from the chair my wife was rocking in. He was tall and well-formed, taller and larger, it seemed to me, than the room allowed. There was power about his person, great power and goodness and patience and love.

I said, "Do you see him there standing beside you?"

Again there swelled that sweet feeling of closeness and unity. She looked at me, confident, a faint smile on her lips. "I don't need to," she said. "I know he is there."

—RICHARD G. ELLSWORTH[1]

The infant that is born on earth brings with it the air of heaven. In its expression, in its smiles, even in its cry you hear the melody of the heavens.

—HAZRET INAYAT KHAN

Her Love Was Heavenly

LIFE IS TREMENDOUSLY EXCITING WHEN YOU'RE READY to be married. I was engaged in April and had plans to tie the knot in July. I worked during the spring and saved up the money I needed for the reception.

In May, I had an unexpected experience. During the night, about one A.M., I was awakened by a voice. It was a girl. She stood by my bed. She was tall and lovely. I immediately knew she would be my first child. It seemed that we already had a deep and loving relationship that I had just forgotten. She expressed tremendous joy at the thought of being able to come to earth and receive a body. She said she loved me. I felt her love was heavenly.

The experience lasted only a few moments. Eight

months after getting married, I became pregnant. I was sick the whole time, but Nycole was born in December 1987. We are now building that deep and loving relationship that seemed so familiar when she appeared that night in May.

—KARRIE B.

It's Time for Me

MOMMY."

I raised my head, listening to hear the voice again, thinking one of my daughters needed something.

"Mommy."

The voice was unfamiliar. I sat up, and to my surprise, saw a figure at the end of my bed. The figure was like a shadow, but all in white, with dark hair and a dark complexion. I shook my head and thought I must be dreaming, but his arms were outstretched, reaching for me.

I thought, "This can't be for real." I reached for my glasses, thinking my eyes were playing tricks on me. Still, there was a child at the end of my bed. I thought, "What do you want?" He spoke to me in a voice that I could hear, but cannot describe.

"Mommy, it's time for me to come."

That's when I realized he was the fourth child I had been promised. Excitement filled my soul, and then he disappeared.

I could not wait to share my great joy with my husband, Ray, who was up early studying for exams. When I shared the news, Ray said, "Cheryl, you just want another child. Don't get your hopes up. There is no way we can adopt a child. We have three girls. And medically, we know you can't have another child."

A short time afterward, Ray was working and had his music playing when he saw a light on in the corridor down the hall. He went to check to see why the light was on. As he walked toward the light, the music stopped and an overwhelming peace came over him. He was reassured that our fourth child was coming.

We began to prepare ourselves and submitted our forms for adoption of a native child. We had applied before in Wetaskiwin and were turned down. We felt there was no point in trying there again, but then my husband felt that we must move to Leduc and try again. This time, to our surprise, everything went quickly and within no time there was a call from Calgary. They had a child and wanted us to come down the following day.

With great excitement, I drove to the school to tell Ray our baby had arrived. When he opened the door, he was not surprised at all. He just smiled and said, "I know."

As we traveled on our way, I felt very impressed that our son should be named Matthew. When we arrived, the social worker met us and made it very clear that this child was a native, that he was very different from us. None of this mattered. All we wanted was the child we already knew.

When the social worker placed him in Ray's arms, I quickly unwrapped the small infant and knew he was our son, Matthew. A shining beam came forth from his beautiful, dark eyes as if to say, "Mommy, I am here. I am here."

My heart swelled, just as it did after giving birth to my daughters.

When the social worker later came to our home to see how we all were doing, she remarked, "You really shouldn't be getting this child. You haven't waited very long, but for some reason your file kept coming to the top each morning. At first I thought it was a mistake, but when it happened again, I felt impressed to call you."

The unknowing social worker simply reconfirmed what we already knew—some things are meant to be. Our family was now complete and united.

—CHERYL CAYER

When my bones were being formed, carefully put together in my mother's womb, when I was growing there in secret, You knew that I was there—You saw me before I was born. The days allotted to me had all been recorded in Your book, before any of them ever began.

—PSALM 139:15-16

Dreams of the Unborn

MY DREAMS HAVE NEVER COME TRUE IN REAL LIFE, except for the two concerning my unborn children. With my first pregnancy, I dreamed three times that my baby would be a boy, blond, born two months early, and perfectly all right. While awake I told myself not even to think about this, as babies two-months premature aren't always "perfectly all right." Yet Simon was born at thirty-three weeks, and was blond and healthy.

Before I even knew I was pregnant the second time, I dreamed that I had twin girls called Jill and Sarah. Later in the pregnancy, I was looking at some pottery "babies" and kept being strongly drawn to the twins. At fourteen weeks gestation, twins were diagnosed, and I said they would be two girls. Sure enough we now have Beth and Sarah (my husband doesn't like the name Jill).

—TRACEY NELSON[2]

He radiated light to bring her forth,
In hidden well—springs, right and left.
The soul descended the ladder of heaven. . . .

— NAHMONIDES

⫻

Irisna's Song

I WAS IN THE MOST BEAUTIFUL PLACE I HAD EVER been.
It happened in a dream, but to me it was fully as real
as the conscious world. Sometime in April 1979, I
had a remarkable visitation in which I met my future
daughter. The location of this rendezvous was filled
with transcending peace. The sun was more golden, the
sky a truer blue, and the grass a greater green than in
my strongest imaginings.

I sat on a park bench in awesomely beautiful surroundings. The radiance of the sun's rays warmed me
from within, rather than on the surface of my skin.
The sounds of the wind and birds and scurrying animals
were hushed, muted, yet simultaneously clear. I felt a
great sense of oneness, connectedness to everything
around me. My senses of sight, sound, and emotion

were all magnified to a greater degree than I had ever felt. The stones, the birds, the trees, the air, all seemed so vitally and vibrantly alive, as if part of some massive cosmic dance. It was an extension of my senses. Surprisingly, all of this seemed normal, as if this is the way things were in the real universe.

Into the midst of this heavenly place there suddenly appeared an extraordinarily beautiful woman. How she got there, or from where she came, I do not know. It felt natural and not at all alarming that she would suddenly appear out of nowhere. In fact, I had no idea how I had come to this magical place.

We sat together at the table-bench, bathed in the surreal beauty of our surroundings. We experienced a wonderful sense of familiarity, as if our souls had danced through eternity with each other. We laughed and talked and communed, all in the stillness of silence.

Yet to use common earth words such as *talked* or *laughed* is incorrect. It is probably more accurate to say that we *thought-felt* together. Our lips did not move, nor did a sound emanate from our mouths. I can't even say that it was telepathy. Telepathy implies that we read each other's thoughts, that I send thoughts to you and you hear them and respond with thoughts of your own. This was more like thoughts being simultaneously realized and exploding in an ocean of thought-feeling-experience in which we were both immersed. Incredible!

We arose from our seats and went for a stroll. Actually, it was more like floating over the surface of the earth with our feet not even touching the ground. Our communication was so all-encompassing that it seemed we covered everything there was to know in the entire universe, and beyond. It felt like a review of things we already knew and were simply recalling, like bringing a long lost friend up to date.

All too soon it was time for us to part company. I knew I was in another world, another dimension, a dream. I wanted something tangible to hold on to so I would remember. So I asked for her name. She whispered melodically, "Irisna." Then she vanished, leaving the name *Irisna* echoing through the corridors of my heart, like a chant, a mantra that mesmerized the totality of my being.

I awakened to the dawn with the melody of the name *Irisna* resonating in my head. I wrote it down and asked the women in my family, including my wife, my mother, and my aunts, if the name *Irisna* meant anything to them. The name was new to them and had no special significance, so I concluded it was not the spiritual name of anyone we knew in this world.

My experience was real, richer than anything I had ever been through in the so-called waking world. I knew in my soul that this relationship, this bond was eternal and I would have future encounters with "Irisna." I looked forward to our next opportunity to enjoy each other's presence.

Over the next several months I had several visitations from Irisna in the dreamworld, and on occasion
in my meditations. Each visitation was as vivid and
real as any conversation I would have in the waking
world. Finally, after several more encounters through
the veil, my last visitation from Irisna took place in
July of 1979. At that time Irisna expressed her desire
to be born into an earthly body. Her thought-feelings
were circumscribed in eternal bonds of familial love as
she asked if I would agree to have her as my daughter.
My response was an enthusiastic and gleeful: "Yes, I
would love to have you in my family." She excitedly
embraced me, telling me I would be contacted later
with further instructions and to just go about my life
as usual. Again she vanished.

I always wondered where she went when she vanished, but I had no power to follow her. She crossed
through an invisible veil that I could not penetrate.
Each time she returned, we rendezvoused in a glorious
realm halfway between the spirit world and the earth
world.

After her last visitation several months passed with
no contact whatsoever. I had become so accustomed to
her visits that I truly missed seeing her and was waiting
with great anticipation for what was to transpire next.

Finally, in late January or early February of 1980
three heavenly messengers appeared as if out of a mist.
They were the most beautiful, angelic creatures I have
ever encountered. They were very tall and elongated,

appearing to be about nine feet in height. Their skin was a smooth, silky, dark brown. They radiated an incredible peace, love, and assurance that rendered me immediately at ease in their presence.

They conveyed to me the message of Irisna's forthcoming birth, announcing that now was the time of her conception. They assured me that everything for her welfare was already arranged—that I would not have to worry about anything financially, logistically, psychologically, physically, or emotionally. All things were already provided for in Spirit; all that was now needed was my consent, my obedience, my follow-through. I immediately gave my consent, responding that I was indeed ready to receive this child as my daughter.

When I awoke the next morning, I told my wife about my announcing dream. Then I asked if she would be willing to go off contraceptives to conceive this heaven-announced girl child. Now, my wife is not a docile, do-everything-that-my-husband-tells-me-to kind of woman. Yet she immediately consented, without so much as a question or resistance of any sort. By her spiritual "in-tuneness" she could feel in her heart that the message I shared of our daughter's readiness to join our family was genuine, a definite directive from the Spirit.

Shortly thereafter my good wife conceived. Nine months later, on November 12, 1980, our daughter was born. We christened her with the same name that she had on the other side, Irisna. I have been unable to find her name in any book of names. However, I intuitively know that Irisna means "she who sees as God sees."

In Irisna's early childhood years she remembered the contacts that we had had in the dreamworld before her birth. As she grew older, the memory of it all faded, until she no longer remembered our prebirth visits. But I know the visitations were real. The memory lives within me. Those visitations are among the most amazing encounters I have ever experienced, and they stand as absolute testimony and confirmation to the existence of life beyond the veil. This I know with a passion, with all the conviction of my heart and soul.

—REVEREND NIRVANA REGINALD GAYLE

There is a constant coming or going
between us and the world of the ancestors . . .
and it's the child who can tell you about
that world since it's coming from there.

—JONATHAN COTT
"Chinua Achebe: At the Crossroads
—An Interview with the Nigerian Writer"

We are only wanderers through the world as in a foreign city, in which before birth we had no part and in this city does but sojourn until he has exhausted his appointed span of life.

—DE CHERUBIM

※

The One Who Brought Me to Earth

I WAS PUTTING THREE-YEAR-OLD JOHNNY TO BED WHEN he asked for a bedtime story. For the past few weeks, I had been telling him of the adventures of his great-great-grandfather: a colonizer, a soldier, a community leader. As I started another story, Johnny stopped me and said, "No, tell me of Grandpa Robert." I was surprised. This was my grandpa. I had not told stories of him, and I could not imagine where he had heard his name. He had died before I had even married.

"How do you know about Grandpa Robert?" I asked.

"Well, Momma," he said with reverence, "he's the one who brought me to earth."

—LOIS P.

And it came to pass that [Jesus] did teach and minister unto the children of the multitude of whom hath been spoken, and he did loose their tongues, and they did speak unto their fathers great and marvelous things, even greater than he had revealed unto the people; and he loosed their tongues that they could utter.

—3 NEPHI 26:14

Taught by a Toddler

I HAD ALWAYS HEARD THAT ONE COULD LEARN MANY things from children, but not until we had a very precious experience with one of our own did I realize how true this could be.

When our first child, Alan, was just past two, his great-aunt Lida passed away. I had been worrying about how I was going to tell Alan about death. My husband and I had taken him to see Lida once or twice a week, so there had to be some explanation for the termination of our visits.

Mustering all my courage, for I was new at this sort of thing, I sat Alan on the kitchen stool and drew up a chair. "Alan, honey," I said, "Aunt Lida has gone back to Heavenly Father."

Before I could say anything more, he asked, "Who took her?" I stumbled around for an answer, and then I said, "It must have been someone she knew."

Immediately his little face lit up as if he recognized a familiar situation. He said with a happy smile, "Oh, I know what it's like. Grandpa Clark brought me when I came to you. He'll probably take me back when I die."

Alan then proceeded to describe his grandfather Clark, my father, who had been dead nearly twelve years. Alan had never even seen a picture of him. But he told me how much he loved his grandfather and how good his grandfather had been to him. Alan indicated that my father had helped to teach him and prepare him to come to earth.

Immediately after this occasion, Alan's father talked to him and Alan repeated the same experience to him. Alan later told his grandmother Clark about the experience. For several months, he talked about these things as a happy, natural memory of real experience. Then, suddenly, the memory was erased and Alan did not know what we were talking about when we discussed it.

However, he had taught us some great truths when he was but a toddler.

—BETTY CLARK RUFF[3]

For I know them and before they came into being I took knowledge of them, and on their faces I set my seal.

—ODES OF SOLOMON 8:16,21

My Father's Hands

IT WAS IN THE LATE 1940S. I HAD FOUR GIRLS ALREADY and desperately wanted a boy, hoping that might secure my faltering marriage. My husband had a hard time relating to all the girls and wanted a son.

After a reasonably normal pregnancy, the final weeks were very difficult and highly stressful. I had no emotional support from my husband, as he was on a job out-of-state and home infrequently. After a long, hard labor alone, I was very tired as the birth time neared. The doctor suggested giving me some medication for pain. I refused, saying, "I have gone this far without it. I'll make it now without it."

In the last stages of delivery, I had an experience I can only call a vision wherein I saw a curtained room. In this room was a long table full of new babies, mostly boys. As I happily reached for one of the boy babies, a man's hands, much like I remembered my deceased father's hands, came through the curtains to stay my reach. Then my father's voice said, "No, no, Bella, not that one, this one," as he placed a baby girl in my hands nearly at the moment of birth.

My father, to whom I was very close, died when I was just thirteen years old. No one else had ever called me Bella.

The baby he handed me was identical to the baby girl I delivered.

—B.T.M.

The child is God's gift to the family. Each child is created in the special image and likeness of God for greater things—to love and to be loved.

—MOTHER TERESA

⤬

The Gift

MY FIRST PREGNANCY ENDED IN A MISCARRIAGE. To everyone's amazement, and to my own, I conceived again only two weeks after the miscarriage. At three months gestation, I experienced another threatened miscarriage with severe cramping and bleeding. We were certain I was going to lose this baby as well. We were all surprised to find during an ultrasound examination that there was still a tiny heart beating within.

Shortly thereafter I experienced a dream in which a beautiful, smiling baby girl with golden hair and blue eyes appeared to me, radiant and bathed in light. The strange thing about this was that I did not feel like I was dreaming, but felt wide awake and very conscious that I was seeing a living being. I remember feeling a very real, loving presence that left me happy and reassured. I was certain after this that I was going to have a girl. And I felt the strongest sense, almost as if I heard a voice, that she wanted to be named Natalie.

When Natalie was born, she looked just like the girl I had seen in my dream so many months before. I came to find out later that Natalie means gift. Surely she is a gift from God.

—NANCY

For as thou hast not forgotten the people who now are and those who have passed away, so I remember those who are appointed to come.

—The Apocalypse of Baruch

⋙⋘

This Is Your Daughter

WHEN I MET MY HUSBAND, WADE, I KNEW THAT HE would make a great father. I also knew that I could not give him children because I had had my fallopian tubes severed when I was twenty-six. Therefore, although I loved him very much and he loved me, I could not marry him until I at least tried to resolve my problem.

I had heard about surgery to reverse a tubal ligation. I had gone to several doctors and they all told me they could not help me because my surgical tubal had been done by burning instead of tying. They said my chances were very low that I would find anyone to correct it. I had seen ten doctors and they all told me they could not help me. While visiting my eleventh doctor, he said, "I can't do it, but I know a doctor who specializes in this procedure, and if any-one can help you, he can."

I called this doctor. It was very hard to get in to see him, as he was booked several years in advance. Luck-ily, I was able to get in after a few months, and the testing began. They found out my hormone level was good and everything checked out—except my eggs could not go down into my fallopian tubes. Fortunately, a small portion of my tubes had not been burnt, so there was the possibility of reconstructive surgery.

I was scheduled for my first surgery. It was a very delicate surgery that was to last seven hours. But during this experience, I stopped breathing. Instantly, I found myself suspended in the air above my body. I could look down and see everything the doctors and nurses were doing. I saw the heart monitor flat and the nurses stirring about. My doctor moved away from me to allow another doctor to come in. I couldn't understand why everyone appeared to be so worried.

I found myself in a place where there was a brilliant white light all around me. As my senses became alert, I heard a beautiful sound—it was the sound of peace. I cannot describe it with mortal words, only that a powerful feeling of peace permeated my very being. I could hear spiritual beings moving around behind me in a very calm and orderly manner. I don't know where it came from, but all of a sudden I was holding an infant. There was a personage behind me and he said to me, "This is your daughter, Virginia."

I looked at her and I was so thrilled. Ever since I was a child I had always wanted a blond-haired, blue-eyed little girl. These were the features of the beautiful baby girl I was holding. My fiancé, Wade, had blond hair and blue eyes.

I looked at her and asked, "Her name is Virginia?"

The personage behind me said, "Yes."

I turned around to thank him, and all of a sudden, the heart monitor started going again and I was immediately returned to my body. I knew I had been summoned back. I was really sad, and my arms hurt because I wasn't holding that beautiful baby.

When I awoke, my doctor was very concerned and he said, "You weren't supposed to do that."

I told one nurse exactly what I had seen her do while I was clinically dead. She was so startled she dropped the tray she was holding at the time. I decided to tell my doctor what had happened. He responded, "I don't disbelieve you. I believe in miracles. I'm a doctor and most doctors I know believe in miracles. But getting back to reality, after that episode we have to wait a considerable amount of time before we dare finish your surgery."

After I recovered and went home, I called his nurse and said, "Every night, after seven P.M., I'm going to stop eating so I can be prepared for surgery if you have a cancellation. I am very anxious to finish my surgery. Please tell the doctor to call me if he has any openings. I'll be ready."

Exactly a month later, they called me. I had the surgery and it was very successful. Two weeks later they did the tests to see if my tubes were open. They were. I proceeded with my plans to marry Wade. I was now very confident that I could give him a child, especially since I had seen little Virginia.

The doctor planned to start fertility drugs in six months. He told me there was no way any fertilization would occur without the drugs. Within three months, I went back to him and told him, "I'm pregnant."

"There is no way you could be pregnant," he said.

"Well, I am," I answered.

"No, you are not pregnant. It is not physically possible for you to get pregnant without the drugs."

It was too early for them to test for pregnancy, so they told me to come back in two weeks, since I had not yet missed a menstrual cycle. In two weeks, I went back. The tests were positive. I knew all along this was my Virginia. We chose Rose for her middle name, after my grandmother.

Virginia was very slow in coming to earth, but she was born healthy, strong, and beautiful—a mirror-image of the blond-haired, blue-eyed infant I had held when my spirit left my body during surgery.

—JoAnn B.

God explains to an unborn soul how it is to descend into matter, and if it will obey the Torah righteously, it will one day return to His presence.

—Tanhuma Pekude

＞＜

A Row of Forms

I HAVE ALWAYS FELT THAT I WAS AN INSIGNIFICANT person. As a young mother, I would listen to women express stories of how the spirit would visit them, in one form or another, as answer to their prayers. I felt I would never be good enough for a spirit to visit me. But one did visit me, many times, as my children were being born.

When my first child was born, I was totally awake because I had had spinal anesthesia. But I had no fear because I had a strong feeling that the child would come early and everything would be fine. I was right.

Twelve months later, I was delivering another baby in a hurry. The only thing there was time for was trialene, a gas that you come in and out of. While I was under, I saw a man dressed in white standing next to my shoulder. He was explaining how spirits get their bodies. In the distance was a row of forms like posts. They were not equally spaced. A couple were fairly close, then there was a slight space and a couple more, and then at a distance another one, and finally, one at the end. He explained that these forms represented spirits coming to get their bodies.

There was a roaring sound that came in rushes, and each time a sound was made, all the forms would move a little closer to us. When the nearest form got right next to us, it was time for that spirit to get its body.

I came to and my baby was born. With all the excitement, I never gave the incident another thought, mainly because I thought the man in white was the doctor or a nurse.

Twelve months later, I was again delivering a baby in a hurry. The gas was given and the man in white was there telling me the same things as before. The forms were coming, though there seemed to be fewer. When I awakened, I again didn't give the experience much thought.

Two years later, our fourth child was being born and the same experience happened again. Twelve months after that our fifth child was born, and I again had the same experience. But this time I spoke to the man in white and said, "Oh, now I understand, there will be more bodies for those spirits."

"Yes, each one is a spirit coming to you," he said.

I was older now and remembered the experience after

I was awake. I thought about the other times I had had the same experience. I realized a spirit had been speaking to me, but I never said anything to anyone.

I had a warm feeling, and I felt as though this man was just trying to help me understand in my own mind the experience of birth, and that there was no need to tell others.

My husband was not in favor of all the children we had, nor did he want any more. He was upset each time I got pregnant. But I felt sure the Lord wanted me to have these children, and He would make sure I did regardless of the contraceptives I used to prevent them.

Four years later, much to our surprise, our sixth child was born. At this time, I was having problems and the doctor and I decided to tie my tubes right after delivery.

But at the time of birth, the same dream occurred again. This time, however, there were only a couple of forms. One was very close, and the other was off in the distance. The man in white and I conversed with each other. I felt very comfortable with him, like we were old friends. There was an excitement watching the forms move gradually toward us with each roaring sound. Finally it was time for delivery, and I said, "But there's one more form."

"Yes, there will be another body for that one." When the sixth child was born, a strange thing happened. The doctor came in and said he didn't want to tie my tubes right then because I was so swollen inside that it would be better if we waited for six weeks. Once out of the hospital, I never went back. Two years later, I went to another doctor and had an IUD inserted.

Four years later, I suddenly got morning sickness—I was pregnant. What a shock. Again it was decided that I should have my tubes tied. When our last little girl was born, the man in white was there. There was only one form coming, and there were no more in the distance. The man said, "That's all of them. There won't be any more." We both smiled and were happy and satisfied. Three hours later, my tubes were tied.

I never once had any regrets or feelings of guilt, as some women do when they decide not to have any more children, because the man in white had shown me I had accepted all the spirits intended for me.

—AUDREY H.

Everything in our life happens as
though we entered upon it with a load of
obligations contracted in a previous existence . . .
obligations whose sanction is not of this present
life, [which] seems to belong to a different world, founded
on kindness, scruples, sacrifice, a world entirely different
from this one, a world whence we emerge to be born on
this earth, before returning thither.

—MARCEL PROUST

Not my planting, But by heaven
My harvest—My own child.

—CAROL LYNN PEARSON
"Beginnings"

≈×≈

Panama City at Dawn

MY DAUGHTER, CARA LANAE, IS NEARLY NINE MONTHS old. Upon reflection, I am astounded at the connection I experienced with her before her physical birth. Prayers, meditation, and dreams led me to my precious heart's desire in awesome, sacred, and mysterious ways.

Our first child by adoption, Cory Rafael, was born September 5, 1990. Our hearts continued to long for more than one child to expand our loving family. From July to December in 1992, two adoption opportunities were presented to us. Through prayer and meditation my husband, Greg, and I were guided not to accept either of them. The grief and letting go afterward felt like a dark cloud, a death of happy anticipation—an "adoption miscarriage." Still, I trusted the divine guidance and the healing process of dealing with my emotions. We took a break from the baby search for the Christmas holidays.

On February 1, 1993, I was guided to take adoption action once again. I wrote a "Dear Birth Mother" letter. My heart was ready for the baby I knew was there. But patience and waiting were the supreme challenges.

During Lent of 1993, I had recurring dreams about a female baby presence. They were more spiritual in nature than visual. One night I even dreamed her name.

I became more diligent than ever concerning the prayer, meditation, and spiritual preparation leading up to Easter. I continually got messages to contact midwives. At first I felt scared and overwhelmed and didn't even know if this was legal. I took no action for a few weeks. But around the first day of spring when Cory (then two and a half) and I were taking a walk on Paynes Prairie amidst the lounging alligators on the riverbanks and the melodious birds happily chirping overhead, the action I was to take became as clear and bright as the Florida spring sun above us. That very afternoon, I called the director of the local birth center to get names of Florida midwives, a list I didn't even know existed. It flowed into my hands with such ease, I felt excited and reassured that this was indeed the correct action to take. The list sat on my office desk for several weeks as I enjoyed the fun and spiritual anticipation of Easter.

On Easter Sunday, April 11, 1993, Greg and I

wrote the "Dear Midwife" letter. The next few days were a flurry of activity as Greg made copies while I stuffed and addressed envelopes. It was exhaustingly tedious, and Cory grew restless at times.

The next night, April 15, in my writing group at church, I wrote a very emotional piece about a birth mother's pain in placing her child up for adoption. Friday night, April 16, I lay in bed exhausted, emotionally and physically. I was sad, wondering when and how I would connect with my baby. I was trying to trust, but it was a very uncertain, stressful period.

That night at eleven P.M., the phone rang. I had an unusual sensation in my stomach. A midwife from Panama City, Florida, was on the line saying that a baby girl had just been born minutes earlier. The birth mom had read the "Dear Birth Mother" letter while she was in labor and wanted Linda, the midwife, to call me. I knew instantly this was the daughter I had been in touch with and was specifically guided to.

We barreled through the dark, Panhandle night for nearly five hours, arriving in Panama City just as the sun was beginning to peek over the Gulf. When I met the midwife at the hospital she said, "It was divine intervention, no doubt about it." She told me they rarely encounter situations such as this, as it is a small hospital.

Cara is now a joyful, curious, expressive, explorative nine-month-old child. She is a very special and precious gift. I am grateful for the connection I had with her through dreams, prayer, and meditation before I held her in my arms. The joyful, feminine energy I felt around her spirit before we met proved to be exactly the essence of her precious personality.

This experience was truly a divine, transformational lesson in faith. I trusted that the right child would be sent to me at the right time and courageously acted on the divine guidance I received. The result is a sweet baby girl and a connection that extends beyond my earthly hopes and dreams.

—SALLY H.

Babies are bits of star-dust blown from the hand of God. Lucky the woman who knows the pangs of birth for she has held a star.

—LARRY BARRETTO
The Indiscreet Years

Too Tiny for Clothes

I BECAME PREGNANT WITH MY FIRST CHILD DURING THE same month I was married. Although neither my husband, Brad, nor I felt right about using birth control and had left our relationship open to receiving a child at any time, the shock of finding I was pregnant so soon was very difficult for me. We had just moved to a state far away from my family and friends, and neither my husband nor I had jobs. We had dated only a short six weeks before our wedding and had many adjustments to make. There were so many things to deal with that I became sick from the pregnancy right away, and was miserably ill for months, not only with nausea but also with bronchitis.

I wanted to be happy about my pregnancy, but I was not. I wanted to feel excited and thrilled to be a mother, yet I had opposite feelings. I found myself constantly plagued with thoughts of death. I felt I should not have the child, that it would be better for me to die than to go through with the pregnancy. These thoughts consumed me daily, and I cried often and very intensely over the morbid thoughts which I found so difficult to control.

One evening during the fifth month of my pregnancy, my husband gave me a blessing and cast away the evil spirit which had been tormenting my mind. In the blessing, I was told that I would have joy with the child I carried within me. I was also told that I would begin to develop a bond with the child that would last through eternity.

That night I had a dream that profoundly influenced my life. I dreamed that I had a baby in my arms. He was so little his clothes kept falling off his tiny body. I was concerned. I didn't know what to do about feeding him because I knew I hadn't given birth to him yet. But as I was trying to care for him, the most wonderful thing happened. We began to communicate with one another with our minds. He was making observations and asking me questions. We were having a discussion. "You and Brad really love each other, don't you?" he asked. I told him that we loved each other very much.

"I'm coming to a good, loving home, and the mistakes made by others in past generations won't be made with me, will they?" I said that we would do our best to make our home loving and caring. I told him we'd do things right and provide him what he needed. He was pleased.

Then he brought up his concern about his physical body. He said he wasn't sure how he'd like it. I told him it would be an adjustment, and I reassured him that it's okay to have a body, and that there would be many things he'd like about it. I told him he'd have pleasures and pains in his physical body.

Shortly thereafter I awoke with the most joyful feeling that carried me through my entire morning. The impressions I had after the discussion with my yet unborn child were that we really had begun to develop a bond that would continue. And though he would be coming to me as a child, I knew his spirit was adult, kind, loving, righteous, and inquisitive.

I knew he would have to learn to live on this earth and deal with the joys and pains of a physical body. Communicating with him was so nice. I felt his personality and the tenderness of his soul. It was beautiful. I will never forget the dream, nor the feelings of joy I had about this child when I awoke.

After the blessing and the dream, I never had a thought about death again, and the joy and excitement of my pregnancy filled my soul. Two months later I had serious complications with my pregnancy, and my son was born six weeks early, weighing only four pounds. But the dream had helped to prepare me for the timing of my son's birth. He was completely healthy. His prematurity, however, did make it difficult to keep clothes from falling off of his tiny body.

—DANA OSGOOD

The Gospel of Philip quoted Jesus: "Blessed is he who is before he came into being. For he who is both was and shall be. The highness of man is not revealed, but is in secret."

—NAG HAMMADI TEXTS
Sayings 57–58

When Spirits Meet

IN 1963, I, LIKE SO MANY OTHERS IN MY HIGH SCHOOL graduation class, felt helplessly caught up in the turmoil of Vietnam and other problems of our times. Each of us wondered how the current events would affect us.

In 1966, I met Lee at the university where he was president of the men's chorus. We often double-dated during the school year with Marilyn and her friend Julie. When Marilyn and I were engaged, I told Lee he ought to be thinking seriously about Julie. They always had a lot of fun together and seemed to be a perfect match. Though he liked her a lot, Lee was hesitant to get too involved.

During Spring quarter of 1967, Lee and I both received notices that unless we raised our grade-point averages, we would not be able to retain our student deferments from the draft. We both studied very hard. By the end of the quarter, my grades were high enough, but Lee's were not.

On June 19, 1967, Marilyn and I were married. Lee attended our reception, and Julie was in charge of our guest book.

Lee was drafted and ordered to active duty on August 5, 1967. Lee was such an outstanding soldier that after basic and advanced individual training, he took the battery of tests and applied for Officer's Candidate School. He was accepted, graduated, and then went on to Ranger School in May, 1969, where he was named Officer Honor Graduate.

I continued on at the university. For nearly three years, Marilyn and I had been trying to start our family. We had even been approved for adopting a baby, but eventually turned down the opportunity. Sometime in October 1969, my wife announced that she was pregnant and was due the first of June 1970. We were both so excited and anxious to share our happiness with our friends.

Lee came home on leave in December 1969. I was teaching full-time. I had Lee spend the day with me and talk to each of my classes. He told them about his training and what it meant to him to be a Christian and to be an officer in the U.S. Army. He spoke with conviction and power. Both the students and I were touched.

Lee came over to our apartment after Christmas, just before he was to leave for Vietnam. We ate, joked, talked, and reminisced. When my wife got up and left the room for a minute, Lee turned to me. "Roy," he said, "I've come to say good-bye. I have to go now. I want to thank you for your friendship. I'm going on another mission, only I'm not coming back from this one."

I looked at him intently, trying to understand his meaning, and then I threw my arms around him, hugged him, and thanked him for his friendship.

"Lee, you take care of yourself," I said, "because I won't be far behind you." I was scheduled to be commissioned as a 2nd Lieutenant on March 23, 1970, and I knew I would be trained and sent to Vietnam within the year.

On April 30, 1970, President Richard Nixon announced that U.S. Troops had begun a ground offensive against Communist bases in Cambodia. The U.S. 1st Calvary Division and the ARVN Airborne Division, totaling more than 40,000 troops, launched the operations.

Lee's unit participated in the offensive action. On May 9, his position was overrun. Lee was making his way out to a perimeter position to tend to one of his wounded soldiers when he was cut down by machine gun fire and killed. Because he had been deep in enemy territory in Cambodia, his body did not arrive home until Wednesday, May 20.

During the five days between Thursday, May 14 and Monday, May 18, I had three dreams about Lee on three successive nights. The first night, I saw Lee dressed in white, sitting on a chair, smiling and looking off into a darkened area. I awoke disturbed and couldn't figure out what it meant.

The next night I saw everything I had seen the night before, but as I looked into the darkened area, a small light grew bigger and brighter as it approached Lee. He was still sitting on the chair, only this time he reached out his arms as if to embrace someone. I awoke again and still couldn't figure out what it meant or why I should be having these dreams.

On the third night, I saw everything as I had the two previous nights, only this time within the light that was coming out of the darkened area was a little girl with blue-green eyes and beautiful, radiant, blond hair. She had curls all around her face and was absolutely the most stunning child I had ever seen. She ran into Lee's outstretched arms. He picked her up, placed her on his knee, and began telling her about me, my wife, and our home. Then, with a sudden burst of excitement, I realized he was talking to my little girl. He laughed and joked with her, and she giggled and accepted his teasing. I awoke with tears streaming down my cheeks and realized I had seen the spirit of our unborn baby. Lee had given her final instructions before she was born.

Cherilee's birth announcement appeared in the newspaper on May 19, 1970, two days before Lee's obituary.

One of my most cherished possessions is a picture of our daughter, Cherilee, with blond, curly, bouncy hair and shining, laughing, blue-green eyes; the same little girl I saw with my friend Lee as his spirit was leaving the earth and her spirit was preparing to come down.

—ROY CALDWELL

Whence camest thou? Thine origin?
What art thou doing here? Knowest thou
not that thou art a spark of Deity, struck from
the fire of His eternal blaze, and brought forth
in the midst of eternal burning?

—JOHN TAYLOR

Each newborn child brings the message that God has not lost his trust in man.

—TAGORE

≍

A Letter to My Son

The following is an edited letter from a mother to her son whom she put up for adoption. She wrote it shortly after his birth and handed it to the adoptive parents to give him when he came of age to understand.

MY PRECIOUS SON,
I do not know how you feel toward me and the decision I made about your adoption, but I trust your parents, and they must feel you are ready to know the circumstances of how you came to be. At the time I became pregnant with you, the relationship with my parents was suffering severely because of my negative attitude. I had just turned seventeen.

Eventually, with the greatly needed help of a church leader, I told my parents of the pregnancy, and we proceeded with making plans on what to do. After much counsel and prayer, and after weighing all possibilities, I made the decision to have you and give you

75

up for adoption. Our parents agreed that your father and I were yet too young to marry.

My parents felt I should live with a foster family in another state until after the birth, and arrangements were made. I now understand the wisdom of their decision, but at the time, I was angry and felt as if I was being "put away" to hide their shame. I did not want to go, and as the time for me to leave drew near, I became desperate to find a way to stay at home.

I had always been strongly opposed to abortion, but with these difficult pressures, I found myself thinking about it occasionally, and even considering it. If I could just remove the presence of the baby, I could move on with my life and everything could go on as it had been. No more problem. No fears. No shame. No facing up to my mistake.

The idea of having an abortion actually started to sound like my solution. I really did not want an abortion, but I was feeling desperate. I knew I had to act quickly as my flight was scheduled to leave within a few days. Each clinic I called was unable to fit me into their schedule until well after my flight out of state.

I was emotionally exhausted when I finally hung up the phone. I went into my room, turned off the light, and crawled into bed, where I cried myself to sleep. It has been many years since that night, but I can still remember the dream I had as clearly as if it were yesterday.

In my dream, it was a few weeks before your sched-

uled delivery date, and I was lying on a table in the
doctor's office having an examination. The doctor
wanted to make sure that you were growing properly
and wanted to take your weight and measurements. He
made an incision in my abdomen and carefully removed
you from my womb. I watched as he had you weighed
and measured. Everything was just fine, and you were
developing normally into a fine, healthy baby. I was
enjoying the experience, yet at the same time I was still
searching for a way in which I should not have to
follow through with the whole ordeal. For a moment,
I considered telling the doctor not to put you back into
my womb—to stitch me up and just let me walk away.

But at that moment, a wonderful thing happened.
You suddenly turned your head and reached out for
me, your big eyes glistening with tears. I could not
resist the urge to pick you up. As I held you close, you
wrapped your tiny arms around my neck with the
strength of an adult and would not let me put you
down. I could feel your desperation to cling to life, and
I knew then that it was a small sacrifice for me to
provide that life for you. The doctor and his office
slowly faded away, and you and I were left alone, still
clinging to each other.

When I awoke the next morning, I told my mother
about the dream. I told her that now I knew without
a doubt that my child had a right to live—a right to
be born into this world and experience the joys, as well

as the sorrows, that this life can bring. My sweet son, please believe me when I say how much I love you!

I thought over every possible solution concerning my keeping and raising you myself, but there were just too many factors mounted against it. I prayed to keep you, but I never felt good about it. I know I made the right decision in having you adopted, but it is the hardest thing I have ever done. You were such a beautiful baby, and I loved you so much.

I felt that another couple that was prepared to start a family, but could have none of their own, would be able to provide for you far more adequately than I. With me, your life would start in shame, guilt, sorrow, and without a father to love you as your adoptive father now loves you.

I truly believe that we are, in some way, assigned children in our pre-earth existence. At one point as I deliberated, I wondered if I might be giving up one of my assigned children by placing you up for adoption. But before I reached a conclusion, I had another thought. What happens to the children assigned to a couple who are physically unable to have any of their own? The moment I had that question, it was answered in my mind. The couples adopt them. Each time the child seems to fit so perfectly into the family. I then realized that I was actually carrying a child that had been assigned to another couple. I hope you understand. Even though I am the person who carried you and gave you birth, your mom and dad are actually your true parents.

Though all my wishes are that I could watch you grow up to be a handsome young man, I know deep in my heart that I have done the right thing. I hope someday in the eternities we may meet and share our feelings face to face. I love you son, and always will.

Forever my love,
MOM

He is the Father of our spirits; and if we could know, understand, and do His will, every soul would be prepared to return back into his presence. And when they get there, they would see that they had formerly lived there for ages, that they had previously been acquainted with every nook and corner, with the palaces, walks, and gardens; and they would embrace their father, and he would embrace them and say, "My son, my daughter, I have you again;" and the child would say, "O my Father, my Father, I am here again."

—*Journal of Discourses* Vol 4:268

⤛⤜

The Choice Was Mine

AT AGE SEVENTEEN, I WAS ON THE REBOUND FROM A failed romance. In desperation, I turned to a fellow who turned out to be very controlling and abusive, both physically and emotionally. I was truly afraid of him. Though I wanted to get away from him, I did not know how. He watched me constantly.

One day we were in the car, exiting a freeway. He became very violent. As he slowed the car down for a stop sign, on an impulse I bolted from the car, vaulted over a fence, and ran across a field where I could hide in the trees and the brush. It was dark and he could not find me.

I was terribly distressed. I knew my life was pointless. It had no meaning. I had existed for two years just to fight and be beaten by this man. I began to consider ways to end my life as I hid in the woods. I did not want to go back to the horrible situation I was living in. Suddenly, I heard an audible voice, as clear as I have ever heard anyone, say: "It is not just your life to consider anymore." I was so startled. I turned to see who had spoken. No one was present anywhere. Again the voice spoke to me: "There is more to consider— there is another life for you to think about." Surprisingly, even though I was hearing a voice while all alone in the woods, I was calm. I knew there was someone kind and unseen watching over me. I again had hope. My life was saved.

However, I did not understand the message. The abusive man, by whom I had been victimized for two years, was ten years older than I. He had lived with another woman for several years previously, and although she tried, she had never become pregnant. After she left him, she immediately became pregnant by another man. So I had assumed there was no way I could have a child by this man. Four weeks after receiving the message from the voice in the woods, I finally understood. I was with child.

Throughout the pregnancy, I felt the spirit of the child within me. I knew the child inside me was a leader and a teacher and had a lot of wisdom. I tried to convince the father to change. But we fought continually for two months. One day, we were in the car, fighting over a hamburger, when something came over me. It was as though someone flipped a switch and a light turned on in my mind. I thought, "What am I doing here? I don't want to be with him. Why am I allowing him to abuse me? Who is he?" He seemed a total stranger to me. I got out of the car, walked away, and never looked back. He didn't even try to follow me. It was over.

I went home to my parents. They arranged for me to go away to a foster home because they wanted me to put the child up for adoption. The family I moved in with had an incredible spirit of love in their home. They loved me completely. They were kind and caring, and I had much time to think in that peaceful environment. I was eight months pregnant and the thought of giving up my child tore me up inside. But what would happen if I kept this child? Could I provide for it?

I had begun seeing a counselor who was very supportive of me. He said, "If you don't know what to do now, I feel you will know whether to keep the child when it is born." In the meantime, a male friend whom I had known for eight years, came home from school. When he discovered my condition, he was very kind and understanding. Our friendship was immediately renewed. Later, he told me that at the time, he had begun to pray that I would keep the child.

The last few weeks before giving birth, I prayed many times daily to know what to do for this child. One night, I had a dream. I was taken into a heavenly realm. There was a park with trees, a beautiful waterfall, golden flowers and an intense, celestial light. I saw three children standing together, with two more standing a little behind them. Of the three, one was tallest. Height seemed to depict age. I knew these three children were mine, and that the other two could be.

I asked the three children, "What should I do? Should I keep this child?" The oldest child stepped forward and said, "It really doesn't matter, just as long as I get to earth." I knew then I was talking to the spirit of the child I was carrying. The child was non-judgmental. She just wanted to come to earth. She again told me she would be fine with either plan—to keep her or to give her up for adoption. She was very calm, and talked to me for what seemed like a very long time. Three times she delivered the same message. The choice was mine.

I awakened feeling very peaceful, but still did not know what to do. Within a few weeks, I went into labor and experienced an unusually smooth delivery as I gave birth to a baby girl. The doctor wiped her off, wrapped her in a blanket, and as he laid her in my arms, she looked up at me and said, "Mama," so clearly everyone in the room heard it and was amazed. All present knew I was considering giving this child up for adoption. As I looked at this beautiful baby who had just called me

"Mama," it was as though I saw myself coming into the world as a brand-new, innocent human being.

The baby was sucking her fists. She wanted to nurse, but they would not let me nurse the baby until I decided whether or not I was going to keep her. They came and took her out of the room, and I was advised I had to make a choice. Then, they left me alone.

I began to pray. I saw myself on a road with a fork in it. I was an older, successful businesswoman in an elegant office. But I was unhappy and unfulfilled. Then I saw myself as a young mother with the child I was considering giving up. We were poor, but happy. I understood my choice. I chose to keep my child.

Seven months later, I married my friend of eight years who had prayed I would keep my child. He has been a wonderful, sweet father to my little girl, loving her as his own.

My little girl is now ten years old. She is loving, helpful, and wise beyond her years. She has three younger siblings, a loving father, and a mother whose life now has meaning.

—NAME WITHHELD BY REQUEST

The Spirit itself beareth witness with our spirit, that we are the children of God.

—ROMANS 8:16

⚍

Our Grandson

IN 1981, I HAD A SPIRITUAL EXPERIENCE THAT BEGAN while I was standing at the kitchen sink washing dishes. The voice of the Lord spoke to me telling me to call my daughter, Michele.

I responded, "But, Lord, Michele is in class."

The Lord repeated his words more strongly, "Call Michele!"

I obediently dried my hands, went to the telephone, and dialed her number at the dorm. To my surprise, she answered the phone.

"Michele," I said, "the Lord told me to call you. Are you all right?"

After a pause, she answered, "I think I am pregnant."

I comforted her and told her I was sorry. We talked a while longer.

After we hung up, I prayed and asked the Lord if

He would terminate this pregnancy. He said, "No. This baby will be very talented and a great blessing."

Our daughter, Michele, was our first child. She held a very special place in her father's heart, and I was concerned how he would take the news. He was soaking in the bath when I went to tell him, so I sat down next to the tub. I proceeded to tell him about Michele's pregnancy and told him that she would be coming home for a few days to rest and regain her bearings. He was obviously concerned about Michele, but disappointed by the news.

I begged my husband, "When Michele comes home, please don't say that you are disappointed in her."

When Michele arrived home, my husband greeted her in his usual way, giving her a hug and a kiss. Then he stepped back and said, "Michele, I am disappointed."

I was worried that she would be hurt, but she responded, "Daddy, I would have been disappointed if you had not said how you feel."

Since those tender experiences, our wonderful grandson, Joshua, has joined our family. He is very talented and a great blessing. He plays the trombone and tuba in the honor band. He sings with and is a soloist for the select choir. He has perfect pitch and a voice like that of an angel.

—RUBY WASHINGTON
1992 National Mother of the Year

We are just raindrops trying to get back to the source, the place from where we came.

—DANNION BRINKLEY WITH PAUL PERRY
Saved by the Light

The Castle Where Jesus Lived

ROD AND I WERE MARRIED MARCH 15, 1979. HE HAD two children, Brandon, age five, and Nicole, age three, from a previous marriage. We chose to have a child together several months later. Terra is thirteen years old now, and she has a very strong testimony of Jesus.

Two years, four hours, and thirty-two minutes from Terra's birthday, our fourth child, Chad Clifford was born. Chad was a colicky baby. He also caught colds frequently. It seemed we were homesteading at the doctor's office. In October of 1982, Chad was admitted to the hospital with pneumonia. He recovered, but my stress mounted.

In November 1983, our daughter Nicole was shot in the neck during pheasant-hunting season. It wasn't serious, just very scary. She was eight years old.

I became depressed. My husband was gone a lot building our new home two miles to the north of our two-bedroom apartment, and I was trying to deal with "left over" problems from my childhood. But on December 22, I had a dream that would later change my life.

I recorded it in my journal—December 23, 1983.

Last night I had a dream about a beautiful girl. I was in a room with a lot of portraits in it. I knew they were portraits of my relatives. I recognized my great-grandma Watts, who lived only a short time after I was born; my Aunt Adele, who is still alive; and my sisters. They were also portraits of my daughters, including one I didn't recognize.

I turned to a woman who I thought was my aunt, but I don't remember her name, only that she had long black hair. I said, "Who is this little girl?"

"This is your daughter, Jessica," she replied.

I had no daughter named Jessica. But as a result of the dream I knew I had one waiting.

In 1984, I received a $1,500 scholarship from Chevron to attend college. I went to school for two years and finished my degree in journalism.

Three years later, in April of 1986, I had all but forgotten about my dream. I was driving home with Chad, who was now four years old. Chad always rode in a car seat in the front. We would talk about his day and what he was feeling.

We exited the off-ramp of the freeway when Chad said, "Mommy, there's the castle."

"What castle?" I asked.

"The castle where I lived before I came and lived with you," he responded.

"Tell me about the castle," I quizzed.

"It's really pretty. Jesus lives there. I used to watch you and Daddy and Bruffy (Brandon) and Nicki and Terra from there. Mommy, my little sister is watching from the castle and she's crying. She fears you're going to forget her. She's waited a long time to come to our family, and she's afraid you're going to forget her," he said.

I was stunned.

Rod, my husband, came home that same night and asked me to have another baby. He said he had felt for a long time that another child was ready to come to our family. I was upset because I didn't really want a baby and I felt God and my family were turning against me.

I went downstairs and dusted the bookcase and came across my diary. It opened to the December 23, 1983, entry. I read, then prayed, and knew my little girl would be coming soon.

Two months later we had a family discussion up in the mountains while camping, after I graduated in June 1986. We asked the kids how they felt about me having another child. They were all excited. Brandon thought we should name her Jessica. Nicole wanted to name her Jennifer. But Terra came up with Jennica, the combined name, and Chad seconded it. Boys names weren't even considered.

In October of 1986, I conceived. I knew it was my daughter, although Rod kept saying it was a boy.

Jennica Sherrie was born on June 17, 1987.

When Jennica began talking, she talked often about her grandma Liz. Sometimes I would catch her talking to Grandma Liz when she thought no one was watching. She would always say, "Well, Grandma Liz said this," and "Grandma Liz said that."

I asked her once what Grandma Liz looked like. Jennica described her as an older woman with long, black hair.

In June of 1991, we went camping by a lake and spent some time with Rod's parents. It was too cold to play in the water, and it was cloudy. So I took the kids and Rod's mom to a nearby cemetery. This one was exciting to us because I knew we had relatives buried there, and we'd never visited it.

As we got closer to the cemetery, Jennica, who was now four, began squirming and said several times, "Grandma Liz, Grandma Liz."

As I opened the door and got out of the truck, Jennica leaped past me and was gone, running through the cemetery.

I followed her. She ran straight to a headstone with

the name Elizabeth Kearl. The headstone showed her picture—a woman who was trying not to smile, with long, black hair wound up in a bun. She looked like the "aunt" in my dream eight years earlier. "I love you," Jennica said. Jennica knelt down in front of the picture and rubbed it tenderly.

She turned to me and said, "Mama, Grandma Liz is in heaven."

After that day, Jennica never talked about or to Grandma Liz. Two weeks later, while helping me with the dishes, she looked out the window and started waving.

"Why are you waving?" I asked.

"I'm saying good-bye to Jesus. He's in his castle," she responded.

"What castle?"

"The one I lived in before I came to live with you. I'm glad you didn't forget me," she said as she happily continued to wave.

—LORETTA P.

Furthermore we have had fathers of our flesh which corrected us, and we gave them reverence: shall we not much rather be in subjection unto the Father of spirits, and live?

—HEBREWS 12:9

I Spoke Another Language

OH, DEAR, WHERE AM I? IT IS SO CROWDED AND DARK here! What am I doing here?"

"Be patient, don't fret; the time is not long and soon you will start on this very important mission of life," a soft voice answered.

"Will you be with me?"

"For a little while." How kind and sweet and reassuring her voice was. "You will become very busy learning all about your new home, and soon you will forget this life and the language we speak."

"Oh, no. I won't forget! I know we have been told we will forget, but I will never forget you, and I will try very hard to never forget how to talk with you."

"This is the way Father says it must be." The soft

92

voice continued. "This family will love you very much, and they are so anxious for you to come."

"I will not be afraid if you are with me."

I discussed many things with this wonderful person with the soft, gentle voice. Fear seemed to leave me as she spoke of this "new life" and how wonderful this "new experience" was going to be for me. She had said, "We must all experience this new life so we can know if we will keep Father's commandments." It seemed that time was endless . . . but soon again the voice spoke telling me that it was time.

It was a Sunday morning, about nine-thirty A.M. The day was beautiful. Warm sunlight flooded the room where I lay next to my mother. The voice said this person was my mother. She smelled so pleasant and sweet, and it was so comfortable to be near her. The light was bright, and I didn't want to open my eyes. I was being passed from one person to another, and they all looked me over. It was such a pleasant feeling to be back safely in my mother's arms again. The people made funny noises and talked strangely—and I didn't understand what they were saying. Lonesome feelings flooded over me, and I cried as if my heart would break. My mother comforted me, talking to me, and soon I felt better. Others picked me up and took turns holding me. I preferred to have the girls hold me rather than the boys . . . the girls were softer. But I couldn't understand what they were saying, and I would cry.

"Why are you so lonely?" the voice asked.

"Because they speak a different language and I can't understand them."

"Soon you will understand, and you will forget this language that you speak," she comforted me softly.

"No, no. I will never forget this language or you."

"Yes, you will forget, and you must try hard to learn what they say. Now I must go, and I will not be coming back again."

"Oh, please come back, please, just one more time." I felt I couldn't bear not to have her close by me. She said she would come back one more time. Once more the voice did return, and I pledged again not to forget her or the language we spoke together.

For a long time I did remember the former language and would compare the words of her language with my new language. Then, I became so excited and involved with all the new, wonderful things I was learning, and with the love for my mother and father and brothers and sisters, that I couldn't take the time to compare, and remember, but this I know, there were two different languages and at one time, I knew them both.

The above experience is true. It was brought to my remembrance as I prayed for guidance in writing my life's story.

—GWENEVERE D. HULSE

A child of Earth and Starry Heaven
am I,
but of Heaven is my true race.

—ORPHIC (Greek) saying, 500 B.C.

Eternal Memories

By PROFESSION I AM A MANAGEMENT CONSULTANT
and a technical writer. The memories I describe herein,
eternal memories, have been with me *all* my life.

My earth body was born on September 11, 1939,
the day that Hitler declared war on Poland. I was
born into a family of southern aristocracy in Jack-
sonville, Florida. The first six years of my life were
spent in my grandmother's house in the country. It
was one of those sturdy, old-fashioned houses built
around the turn of the century, situated on roughly
fifteen acres of land. French doors opened out from
the drawing room toward Mother's bedroom. The ad-
joining sitting room served as my bedroom for several years. It contained my wooden cradle and a
rocking chair that was very special to me. But I am

getting ahead of my story. Let me go back to an earlier memory . . . before conception.

Although the process is difficult to describe in earthly terms, my memory extends back to previous realms of existence, before earth life. Similar to mortality, I recall experiences of growth, learning and development in the realms before earth life. My growth experiences there brought me into a time when I knew I must depart the cosmic spiritual world, a kind of graduation if you will, in order to progress in a new realm.

When my departure was imminent, I found myself poised as if at the edge of a vast and bottomless abyss. The Exalted Ones waited patiently, offering me time to launch myself by my own will. I aspired to make the leap of faith, but my courage wavered as I teetered between the two worlds: the familiar home I was leaving and my new earth home somewhere out there in the vast, foreboding universe that stretched before me.

Finally, the Exalted Ones could wait no longer; my earth mother was ready for me. I felt a gentle but firm push. From a state of immense expansion in spiritual cosmic space, I felt myself falling and contracting at what seemed to be the speed of light. At some point, consciousness temporarily slipped away.

I awakened in a kind of dreamy state and found myself encased in a cloudlike body (more dense than my spirit body), enveloped by and peacefully floating in the radiant presence of a new being. I felt comfortable and protected in the spiritual warmth and physical strength of this being. I was in the womb of my earth mother.

From time to time I heard inner speech, spiritual tones that formed shapes in my mind and resounded in color. I came to realize that I was being taught the language of my new environment and that the spiritual organs of human feeling and thinking were being formed within me. I was not yet fully aware of the physical world, but I could feel my cloud-body becoming denser and more human in form.

After several weeks of earth time, I became conscious through my cloud-body (fetus) of a spiritual being next to the radiant presence (my mother). I know now that this spirit-being was my great-grandfather Apollus. As my cloud-body densified (grew) and I became more conscious through it, Great-Grandpa also manifested his human form more densely within his auric field. I remembered Great-Grandpa Apollus from the life before earth life. Following his death, he returned home to the spiritual world where we enjoyed many wonderful times together before my departure to earth. I was grateful to feel my great-grandfather's love again, for the transition from heaven to earth can be a shock.

From time to time Great-Grandpa Apollus continued to visit me. He held me lovingly and rocked my spirit-form baby body in the old wooden rocking chair as he taught me English. He prepared me for human existence by "speaking" words into my soul, which were accompanied by pictures and symbols with inward meaning. This gave me a collection of words, phrases, and concepts in the English language that enabled me to recognize physical objects and understand spoken language when I acquired full physical consciousness.

At last the day arrived when I burst fully into physical awareness. At my birth, the door to the spiritual world, our eternal home, closed behind me. I found myself clothed in a body of flesh, a physical being in a world of physical beings. I could no longer contact my beloved Great-Grandpa Apollus! I now had to summon all of my courage and face this harsh new physical world, imprisoned in a tiny body and at the mercy of larger beings . . . dependent upon them for survival.

Although I understood English from birth, having received language training during the visits from Great-Grandpa Apollus, I did not speak aloud for many months. The prebirth lessons from Great-Grandpa Apollus had equipped me with the faculty of silent speech, so I was able to vocalize my thoughts intelligently once I learned to direct my physical voice. At eighteen months of age, I remember crawling on the floor, feeling lonely, looking up and seeing how large the other human beings were compared to myself. I missed Great-Grandpa Apollus even more urgently than usual. So, to everyone's surprise, I vocalized my thoughts for the first time:

"Where is the man with the beard? Where did he go?"

The adults were stunned. At the time I knew nothing about Great-Grandpa Apollus's earth identity. He had died in 1924, fifteen years before my birth. I knew him only as the radiant presence who helped me to incarnate into human form.

As I ponder that moment when I first spoke aloud, I realize how it must have startled everyone present for an eighteen-month-old child to suddenly show a dramatic change in awareness and begin to speak whole sentences in perfect English. Well, I kept pestering everyone for days, repeatedly asking for the "man with the beard." I was desperate to see Great-Grandpa Apollus again. To appease my requests, I was shown numerous photographs from family albums. Each viewing resulted in the same response, "No. That isn't him."

The experience was probably as frustrating for my new family as it was for me. They no doubt thought I was referring to someone I had seen in the household, so initially I was shown pictures of people still living. Bearded relatives and friends were rare. One day, as a last resort, my mother pulled out a portrait of her long-dead grandfather. He had a beard. Instantly, I recognized the picture of Great-Grandpa Apollus. I was ecstatic. You see, I believed by identifying him, my family would find him for me.

I excitedly pointed to the picture. "That's him. That's him. He's the one who held me. Where is he? I want him to come back."

Mother stammered, "That's impossible. You couldn't have seen him. He's been dead for years!"

At the time, Mother did not understand. But I have known all my life I was nurtured and trained by my deceased great-grandfather as I made the transition from the cosmic spiritual world to the human condition of earth life. This is but a small portion of my "eternal memories."

—KIRK D. GARDNER

We say "All this hath been
        before,
All this hath been, I know not when
        or where."
So, friend, when first I looked
        upon your face,
Our thought gave answer, each to
        each, so true,
Opposed mirrors each reflecting
        each—
Altho' I knew not in what time or
        place,
Methought that I had often met
        with you,
And lived in each other's mind
        and speech.

> —ALFRED, LORD TENNYSON
> *"Early Sonnet"*

Jesus said, "If they say to you, from where have you originated? say to them, we have come from the Light, where the Light has originated through itself. If they say to you, who are you? say, we are His sons and we are the elect of the Living Father."

—The Book of Thomas (Logion 50)
Nag Hammadi Texts

My Angel Wrapped in Light

I WAS FIVE AND A HALF MONTHS PREGNANT WITH MY third child. The doctors discovered gallstones blocking my bile duct. Doing immediate surgery, they saved my life and I was out of danger. The surgery took many hours and was very difficult. I bled heavily, and for a few seconds my heart stopped. My husband was told that there was little chance that the baby would survive. One difficult night after the surgery, the nurse was performing a routine check of the baby's heartbeat. She could not find it. She checked for over half an hour and finally called a nurse and doctor from the maternity floor. They checked for over an hour. I was told that they felt the baby had died, and they started to

1 0 3

set up an ultrasound to verify it. They left to call my husband and my doctor.

Alone in the darkened hospital room, I poured out my heart to the Lord. My heart grieved for the baby I had never held, the smiles I had never seen, the steps never carefully counted. As I pleaded with the Lord for strength and peace for my spirit, I fell into a deep sleep.

I dreamt that I was at the bottom of a flight of white steps. Around me were my husband, two sons, parents, sister, brother, and departed loved ones. I heard my name called and looked up to the top of the staircase. There was a throne surrounded by a light and a figure standing before the throne. A feeling of great love, compassion, warmth, and calmness entered my spirit. I climbed the stairs and knelt on the step below his feet. I bowed my head in reverence and awe. Suddenly hands descended into my view. In these beautiful hands rested a shining baby wrapped in white. I gazed into crystal blue eyes with beautiful black lashes. She had dark black hair, and as I gazed, she smiled at me. I began to cry from joy and amazement.

Then I heard these words, "I give this child to you to raise for me. She is a gift that someday you will return to me. She is my little sister and is very beloved. Teach her of my love. Show her my example. Help her find me and my path. I died for her and for the chance to bring her back to Father. Behold, the precious gift I give to you."

The light grew and suddenly I knew her. I received

glimpses of long ago and promises made. I yearned to keep those promises and to hold my precious gift.

The bundle was placed in my hands, and my tears dropped to the white blanket. I felt awed and amazed at this great trust in me. How could I ever be worthy of this beautiful gift? I slowly walked down the stairs and stood before my husband. I held out my arms, and he gently took the angel of light from me.

I suddenly woke up when the doctor returned. I told him to check the baby again, because I knew she was alive and strong. He agreed and on his first try found a strong, regular heartbeat.

Three months later I gave birth to a seven-pound-six-ounce baby girl. She had crystal blue eyes, dark black hair, and looked exactly like the baby in my dream. As I gazed into her eyes, I saw again my angel wrapped in light.

—DEBBIE C.

And it shall come to pass in those days
that the elect and holy children
will descend from the high heaven,
and their seed will become one
with the children of men.

—1 ENOCH 39:1
Old Testament Pseudepigrapha

Dream Boy in the Garden

IT HAPPENED IN AUSTRALIA. THE MOMENT I SAW MY
little boy, I fell completely in love with him. He was
so adorable with his blond hair curling about his angelic
little face. I remember so clearly how it felt to look
into those pure little eyes and experience his gaze of
incredible wisdom. The desire to pick him up and en-
fold his little body in my arms and hug him to me
grew in my heart. There and then we forged a bond
that I knew would last forever. He continued on with
his play and danced out of sight across the beautiful
meadow, leaving me to wonder if I was awake or asleep.

As I lay in my bed half awake, my mind contemplated the vision I had just experienced. The scene came

again of the child in a lovely garden from which ema-
nated feelings of peaceful happiness. The very flowers
and grasses swayed in harmony, as if blown by a gentle
breeze filled with soft music. Into this peaceful scene,
the figure of the little child came dancing, as though
from the wings of a theater stage. Although he was
moving quickly, his movements were in total harmony
with his surroundings. He seemed completely comfortable there. He continued to play and dance, softly
laughing as children do when they are totally absorbed
with their amusements.

I watched, fascinated by the beautiful picture I was
observing. The child moved closer to me, and I could
see that he was a little boy with fair hair. The breeze
would catch little tufts of his hair and move them
slightly as he ran back and forth across the garden.
Then, when he was quite close to me, he stopped and
looked at me, and that was when our eyes met. And
though he never spoke, we had a complete understanding of the love that passed between us.

Now into my fully awake mind came thoughts that
were so clear there could be no confusion. This little
boy was an unborn child that was awaiting his turn to
come into this world. I was to be his mother, and it
was my responsibility to see that he did not have to
wait much longer. When he was born I was to name
him Andrew, because his name had already been
chosen.

Having basked in the splendor of this vision, I then

remembered some grim realities. We already had seven children, and my husband had, only a few days before, made it very clear that our family was complete and that there would be no more children. I had agreed, even though little stirrings of maternal love had been tugging at me.

The other problem was much more acute. To my sorrow, a rift was growing between my husband and me. He was working later in the evenings, and his extra activities took him away more and more from the family. My life was filled with the daily chores that accompany a large family living on a farm in Australia. We were also very active in church and community affairs. There was not much time for self-pity.

This was not an ideal time to tell my husband about my dream-vision, or to express my desire that we have another child. So I kept these things to myself and wondered what I could do to see that beautiful little boy I knew was waiting to come to me.

There was only one time that whole month that we were intimate enough to conceive a child. But the miracle happened, and I was pregnant. It was a difficult pregnancy, and there were even times when I feared that I would miscarry. The last three months, I was confined to bed and could hardly walk because of a separated pelvis. Despite the problems, I delivered a healthy baby boy. I was allowed to name him Andrew.

When Andrew was six weeks old, my husband sent

the eight children and myself on a cruise through the South Pacific to America. He accompanied us to Fiji, then flew back to Australia, because he could not leave his business affairs longer than the week he had spent on the ship. We continued on and disembarked in Los Angeles, where friends met us and got us settled for the night. For several days we had a great time seeing the sights, visiting Disneyland and all the attractions to which the children had been looking forward.

During the month that followed, I did not think about my dream of Andrew because my life was filled with events that used up all my thoughts and energies. I soon discovered that when my husband sent us on this trip, he had really been sending us away. He deserted us and left us to sort out our own lives, because he was busy building a life with another woman. The story of our survival is a miracle in itself.

The children and I stayed in America, and I eventually remarried. My new husband adopted all of the eight children, and we settled down to a wonderful life.

One lovely spring day, I was looking out the large picture window that overlooked the lawn in the backyard. Andrew was playing by himself in the grass— happy in the warm sunshine. He was about three years old, with blond hair and blue eyes. He stopped for a moment when he saw me looking at him, and our eyes met through the glass. I saw a look of pure happy love in his eyes. Instantly the dream that I had had before he was born came to my mind, and I recognized the identical child from that beautiful garden in my dream.

Someone, somewhere knew that events in my life were taking such a turn that Andrew had to come then, or who knows when . . .

—JEAN H.

As the eye of man reaches the stars where it had its primitive origin, so the soul penetrates and sees even within the divine state of being wherein he lives.

—JACOB BOEHME

Kidnapped

October 7, 1986 STARTED OUT AS AN ORDINARY Tuesday in our home. Stacy and Robert went to school. My husband, Mark, went to work.

At 1:45 P.M., I called Mark. "I don't know how to tell you. . . ." My voice trailed off. "Something terrible has happened." I paused. "Oh, Mark . . . They've taken Sarah!"

I had been watching our preschool children and a neighbor boy. Suddenly the phone rang. It was Robert. He needed me to go to the school. Gathering all the children in the car, I headed out. When I arrived, I ran in and took care of Robert and came back out. When I returned to the car, the five-year-old neighbor boy innocently looked at me and said, "A man took Sarah out of the car."

"That's not funny. Stop playing around," I scolded.

Again, with a serious face and big eyes he said, "A man took Sarah out of the car."

This time I knew he was not teasing. I could not see my precious three-year-old anywhere.

Returning to the school office, trying not to panic, I reported the incident. Soon the nurse, the principal, and other office ladies were right there to help. "I left Sarah and the other kids in the car unprotected," I lamented to myself. My mind blurred. I could not remember Mark's work number, so the office ladies looked it up in the file and called him. Rushing to the school, Mark found the police already there, trying to get the story straight from me. I could not believe that this was really happening.

The principal took the children home, and a church leader's family fed and took care of them while my husband and I went to the police station. We answered questions for the police and the F.B.I. late into the evening. "Do you know anyone who might want to take Sarah?" We could think of no one.

We silently prayed that the Lord would help and protect Sarah wherever she was, and give us the strength to endure. It was useless to think of the possibilities of what might be happening to Sarah. We had to trust Sarah to God's hands while we did what little we could. We cried with fear, not knowing if we would ever see her again in this life. Was she hurt? Afraid? Not knowing was the hardest part.

As the children were eating dinner, they asked what Sarah was eating and wondered if the kidnapper was even feeding her. Little Bobby went outside and called "Sarah! Sarah!" until his innocent, quivering voice was entirely spent.

The police said that intense media coverage can scare a kidnapper into letting the victim go. A press conference was held. It lasted about twenty minutes. An outraged and saddened Arizona metropolitan community united their sympathetic hearts and trained their eyes on their televisions as reporters asked us about what happened.

"Help us find Sarah," we pleaded. And to the kidnapper, we begged: "Let our little girl go. Drop her off at a street corner or supermarket or anywhere, and she will be just fine. We just want our little girl back."

Arriving home late that night, exhausted, we found all our children asleep. Turning to the Lord in prayer, we sought help and comfort. Acting as voice at this critical time, Mark was scared that his highly emotional condition and his intense desire for Sarah's safe return might bias his ability to discern true promptings from the Spirit of God. At first, the prayer centered around consoling me—that I was not at fault. Then Mark was also given a glimpse of the anguish of the kidnapper, who surely felt extreme guilt for his act. Mark wanted to assure me that Sarah would be okay, but he couldn't. He was constrained. This frightened him. Just one month prior, he had tried to assure me in a prayer concerning my pregnancy that the baby would be born healthy and well. Then, too, he had been restrained from saying this. I had a miscarriage five days later. Was Sarah not going to be coming home? Why couldn't he form the words?

Mark continued his prayer, grasping for words of comfort by speaking of a loving Heavenly Father who is fully aware of all events. Then his voice seemed to change. It was more of a pure tone and much calmer than his normal voice. His throat, he said, felt different too, almost smooth. The words started to flow spontaneously so that it seemed that he, too, was listening to them. Mark remarked how special Sarah was and that there was much yet for her to do in this life.

Then Mark began weeping as he anticipated what he was being wrought to say next. This lasted for several moments. Finally the composure and the welcome words came: "Sarah is alive and well. She is protected from evil and the deeds of evil men. There are angels attending her and protecting her from harm. There is no power in earth or heaven that can or will harm her. Sarah is good, and good will always win over evil. Sarah will return to you and grow up in your household and be your little girl again." This was followed by tears of joy and rejoicing. Mark understood why he could not say that Sarah would be okay at first. "The first time, I wanted to say the words but couldn't. The second time, the Lord wanted to say them and did."

For us, the trial was already over—just ten long and

lonely hours after Sarah was taken. But the ordeal dragged on for three more days. We talked to numerous news people and were able to tell them that we had full confidence that Sarah would return safely.

Later, we would put together more pieces of the story. While I had run into the school to tend to Robert's needs, Sarah, two-year-old Heather, and the neighbor boy were playing on the seats and hiding on the floor of the car. Sarah was sitting on the driver's seat with the window rolled down. A rough-looking man approached the car. He had long, curly, dark hair with a mustache and beard.

"You're coming with me," he said.

Sarah said, "No."

The man then reached into the car and pulled her out through the window. She did not scream or kick as he carried her to his dark brown truck. He put her in the truck and told her to lie on the floor. It was hard and uncomfortable. He drove for a while without saying a word or listening to the radio. They went on a curvy, bumpy road and stopped. After abusing her badly, he opened the door and she jumped out. She walked away from the truck, and he made no attempt to stop her. He drove away, and she never saw him again. This entire experience with the "bad man" lasted probably less than an hour.

Sarah walked away from the dirt road, went to a bunch of trees and sat down. She did not cry or try to follow the road back to the highway. She just stayed "in the trees." "I just knowed what to do," she later reported. Barefoot and pantless, she was scratched by the cacti and her little feet were sore and punctured as she determinedly walked the long distance to the trees. She knew where to go even though she could not see the trees from the road. She knew she had to stay by those trees and should not move.

When it got dark, she went to sleep. Awaking when it was yet dark, Sarah was alone and scared. She then saw a small child in the desert. The child had short, blond hair and slightly resembled her little sister, Heather. The little girl was wearing a white robe that looked like a T-shirt. She was surrounded or encircled by a brilliant light. Sarah thought the leaves of the trees would catch fire because it was so bright. When later asked how she could see this personage, Sarah said, "In my eyes. She wasn't really in the desert, but she wasn't in my mind either. I didn't pretend. I could see her in my eyes." The shining girl of comfort just stood there and smiled but did not speak to her aloud. Sarah stayed by the trees for two days, as she was constantly attended by her comforting little friend.

Having a premonition that Sarah would return on Friday, we spent Wednesday and Thursday just waiting. We tried to get back to a partial routine. By this time, the whole community was involved and posters were going up all over the state. Over $21,000 in reward money was pledged and is still being offered for the arrest of the abductor. People we did not even know donated thousands of dollars to the reward and offered time and services printing and distributing posters and searching.

Thursday night it rained hard, and it was cold. We prayed that Sarah would be kept dry and warm. Mark said to me, "Rhonda, if Moses could part the Red Sea, the Lord certainly can part a few raindrops for our Sarah."

Sarah was a little hungry and thirsty but did not eat or drink anything. Thursday night, during the downpour, Sarah said the trees protected her, and she did not get wet. She could put her feet out in the rain and pull them back in out of the rain.

Friday morning, Sarah left her place of refuge and began walking. She did not try to retrace her steps, but took a new route. She recounts, "I knowed I had to walk." She said Heavenly Father helped her know which way to go. She walked from early morning until nine A.M., when she heard a loud noise. It was the gun of a quail hunter. Friday was the opening day of quail season. She stood by and waited to see what the hunter (Zane Bingham) would do. He came toward her looking for the bird he shot. When he looked down the wash, Sarah was staring back up at him. Recognizing her from the posters, he picked her up and took her to a restaurant, where she was cared for until an emergency helicopter arrived.

As we awoke Friday, we were filled with hope that Sarah would be found. We drove to the police station to undergo further questioning. While waiting in the hallway, Mark could hear cheering and excitement. He finally heard one lady say, "I can't believe they found that little girl alive." Mark silently cried tears of joy and offered a prayer of thanksgiving. It happened just as we knew it would.

Arriving at the hospital emergency room, we were reunited with Sarah. She was being checked by the doctors. Samples of dirt, sticks from her hair, and dried tears were being taken. She was scratched and dirty from head to toe. At first, she didn't even look like our Sarah, but we knew it was. She didn't respond to us at all. She was in shock and did not say a word. I guess I expected her to be the same as when she was taken and say, "Hi, Mom and Dad. Let's go home." But she had been through a lot and was still trying to figure out what was happening.

Sarah just silently watched what the doctors were doing. Suddenly her countenance changed, and she smiled and said, "I saw Heather playing in the desert," referring to her desert companion. Heather was her youngest sister. We did not understand at the time what Sarah meant. We knew she could not have seen Heather because Heather was with us from the time Sarah was taken.

Sarah went right back into shock and didn't respond to any questions. It really didn't matter. Sarah was back. She spent the next day sleeping and gulping down food and drink. She did not say a word and did not smile.

But the thing that impressed her most through the ordeal was the familiar-looking small child who stayed with her in the desert. The first words she spoke were about this comforting friend who looked like her little sister.

It was Saturday morning when she really started to talk. Sarah's account of the events of those four days was compiled and organized based on statements she made and her responses to questions asked her over the next month. But it would be over three years before the identity of Sarah's shining guardian angel in the desert was discovered.

When we gradually returned to a semi-normal family life, about a year after Sarah's ordeal, a baby sister, Jessica, was born. As Jessica grew, she had blond hair. When Jessica was nearly three years old, Sarah stopped suddenly one day and looked at her little sister intently. Then she became very excited as a look of amazement came over her face. "Mommy," she said, "it was Jessica in the desert. Her hair is the same as it was then. She is the same size now . . . She was my helper. Jessica was my shining friend in the desert!"

—THE SKIDMORE FAMILY

Will you see the infancy of this sublime and celestial greatness? Those pure and virgin apprehensions I had in my infancy, and that divine light wherewith I was born . . . I was a little stranger which at my entrance into the world was saluted and surrounded with innumerable joys. My knowledge was divine; I knew by intuition those things which since my apostasy I collected again the highest reason.

—THOMAS TRAHERNE

Who Are You?

CLEARING AWAY THE MORNING DISHES ON A BEAUTIFUL warm and sunny spring day, I was feeling an amazing contentment with my life. My husband and I had a new home, a beautiful family, and a wonderful marriage. It seemed that we had everything that anyone could want or need.

When the doorbell rang and interrupted my thoughts, I assumed that it was my neighbor. She had phoned earlier in the day about a lost dog and mentioned that she would soon be over. But when I opened the door, there stood a strange man. Before I realized what I had done, I had allowed him into my home. He said he needed to use my phone because of car troubles. I knew immediately that I had placed myself in great danger. Before I had time to think, he was pointing a gun at me. I was in a daze as he proceeded to assault and molest me.

After finishing with me, he locked me in my bathroom. The stranger then ransacked my house. As I contemplated my plight, a feeling of calm came over me and I asked the Lord: "Please, if this man is going to kill me, let it be swift. Please take care of my family, and please carry their grief." My fear totally vanished as I felt a presence beside me. Although I saw no one, the presence was unmistakably that of a young woman—gentle and kind. I said out loud, "Who are you?"

I sensed that this spirit essence was a blood relative, and I assumed that this was a guardian angel that was going to take me to the other side should I be killed. The presence was so powerful that I knew this person was in charge of the situation now, not the criminal. My mind was not on the criminal, although he was still in my home. My mind was on this unseen person who was with me. Finally I heard the intruder leave, and almost immediately thereafter I felt my spiritual friend depart.

I managed to unlock the bathroom door and run outside my house. As the sun warmed my face, I felt so thankful to be alive. I thought, "Thank you, God for letting me live. I will be okay."

I never spoke to anyone about my experience with the unseen comforter—partly because it was very personal in nature. Ten months later, after six and a half years of wanting another child, I was delighted to find myself pregnant. I knew I was having a girl. I told the doctor, my friends, and relatives. There was no doubt in my mind, although many of them teased me for my confidence.

On the night my baby was born, it was almost as if there was an aura of light around her head. All attending were in awe at the miracle of this great occasion.

When the doctor had cleaned her off somewhat and made sure that she was breathing well, he placed her in my arms. It was as though everyone else in the room faded into the background, and she and I were alone. I looked into her eyes and thought, "Who are you?" In response, her little eyes became transfixed on me and we had an immediate recognition. I said, "It was you." No one else knew what I meant, but I knew she did. She was my unseen comforter—my guardian angel. She had been watching me for a long time before her birth.

—NAME WITHHELD BY REQUEST

How like an angel came I down!
    How bright are all things here!
When first among His works I did appear
    Oh, how their glory me did crown!
The world resembled His eternity,
    In which my soul did walk;
And everything that I did see
    Did with me talk.

The skies in their magnificence,
    The lively, lovely air,
Oh, how divine, how soft, how sweet, how fair!
    The stars did entertain my sense,
And all the works of God, so bright and pure,
    So rich and great did seem,
As if they ever must endure
    In my esteem.

A native health and innocence
    Within my bones did grow;
And while my God did all His glories show,
    I felt a vigor in my sense
That was all spirit. I within did flow
    With seas of life, like wine;
I nothing in the world did know
    But 'twas divine.

               —THOMAS TRAHERNE
               "Wonder"

God that made the world . . . hath made of one blood all nations of men for to dwell on all the face of the earth, and hath determined the times before appointed and the bounds of their habitations.

—Acts 17:24,26

✳

Playmates from Heaven

I HAVE EXPERIENCED UNCOMMON DIFFICULTIES BEARing each of our children. In 1973, during the birth of our first daughter, I suffered cardiac arrest. The medical staff worked swiftly. A C-section was performed. Their efficiency saved our daughter and revived my vital signs. We both were favored with a full recovery. But my husband was so shaken by the trauma of those frightening hours that he determined we would have no more children—the risk to my life was too great. You see, my own mother had died when I was ten, so we were very sensitive to the trials of children growing up without a mother.

Nevertheless, I could not overcome the plaguing sensation that our family was incomplete, that somehow more children were assigned to join our family.

When our first daughter, Angie, was about three years old, my father invited us to accompany him on a trip to Washington to visit my sister. We had a nice time. On the return trip, we stopped at a beautiful rest area alongside the highway in Idaho. My father, Angie, and I were the only people present as we relaxed in the peaceful surroundings. A motion caught my eye, and I glanced over toward Angie, only to see her playing with a beautiful red-haired girl, also about age three. Strangely, I was neither startled nor alarmed. The mirthful relationship enjoyed by these two little souls seemed perfectly natural, as though they had always been linked by an unseen but powerful bond. In short, they belonged together.

I was enraptured by this blissful scene for several minutes as the two children played a ring-around-the-rosy type of game. Then their moment of togetherness ceased as the cherubic guest simply disappeared before my eyes. Angie was at peace with both the coming and the going of her little playmate. As I sat pondering this celestial vision, I was filled with a "knowing" that the diminutive redheaded visitor was *my daughter*. Upon returning home, I shared with my husband the miracle I beheld through the veil in the Idaho countryside. I accepted it as a manifestation of the will of God that we receive another gift from Him—another daughter.

The wonder of the incident overcame my husband's fears for my health, and he pledged to honor my desire to bring another child to our family. Our faith was tested as I suffered two miscarriages during the ensuing months. Finally our heavenly gift was born, a beautiful little girl . . . with red hair. When she reached three years of age, she looked just as I remembered her during her heavenly prebirth appearance at an Idaho rest stop.

Due to the threat of miscarriage during this pregnancy, I had been required to spend much of the nine months in bed. Surprisingly, our second child was born naturally—unusual after a previous C-section. As my husband observed me growing stronger, his fears eased. He supported me as I gratefully birthed two more daughters, both C-section. Our fourth daughter was born while we were living in British Columbia, Canada. Between daughters two and three, I experienced the heartache of two more miscarriages. However I was determined to keep trying because I just "knew" we had four daughters in our family.

During the seventh month of pregnancy with our fourth daughter, I had been alone one day looking at photo albums of my ancestors. Suddenly an unanticipated message was communicated directly to my mind, in the fashion described by near-death experiencers who communicate with those on the other side through their thoughts. The missive was, "When you have a son, his name will be Michael." In my heart I believed that my current pregnancy was our fourth daughter, not a son. My belief proved correct, therefore the spiritual message regarding "Michael" foretold a future child.

When I later explained this experience to my husband, he chided, "If we have a son, I don't want to name him Michael. There are already too many people with the name Michael in this world."

I chuckled and responded, "His name came as a message, not a choice. I am not the one who chose his name. I'm just the messenger."

The prospect of a future son was soon eclipsed by the birth of our fourth daughter. But I, in the pattern of Mary of old, "pondered these things in my heart."

It had required much sacrifice, but our four daughters were now here, safely within our family. Shortly after my fourth delivery, the Canadian doctors insisted that I bear no more children, as they felt it would be a threat to my life. They even scheduled me for surgery to assure that I followed their counsel.

Despite the medical facts, I felt much sorrow at the thought of bearing no more children. I anguished over the risk of losing my life and being unable to rear my four daughters. But I also recalled the telepathic message announcing a son named Michael. I was certain in my heart that God was preparing a son to join our family.

Meanwhile, my health deteriorated gradually, making additional children a doubtful part of our future. To avoid the pressures we were feeling in Canada from the medical establishment, we moved back to the United States so I could return to the doctor who had delivered our third daughter. He understood my health problems well, and he was also a spiritual man. When I explained my impression that a son needed to join our family, he did not ridicule me. His response was that another pregnancy would be difficult, but he would help me if I truly felt another child was destined for our family. He knew the high risk but manifested faith, saying, "We will find a way to succeed if it is meant to be."

Following our move back to the States, I managed a small bookstore, while my husband worked in a distant town, which required a commute of about an hour and a half each way. He was unable to find employment nearby. The days were long and taxing for all of us. Although I tried to become pregnant, I could tell my husband was hesitant. He was still fearful he would lose me if I attempted another pregnancy and if I continued refusing the surgery I needed. Things continued this way as I endured three more years of poor health. I was chronically fatigued and wondered if the door would open for Michael to join our family.

In spite of being reluctant for me to bear another child, my husband often had the curious experience of asking in an absentminded sort of way who was missing at the dinner table, even though all four of our children were present. He was always embarrassed when he realized his mistake, but he repeated this scenario from time to time.

Then, God intervened. Again.

It was a typical day at the bookstore. My two preschool daughters were playing in the store as I reviewed receipts and expenses. No customers were present at the time. I was so sick of incessant ill health and the inability to conceive that I finally reached for the phone to call my doctor. I intended to tell him I could suffer no longer, to please schedule my surgery as soon as possible. My heart was truly heavy with this decision. I knew it would signal the end of my childbearing.

As my hand touched the phone, an adorable red-headed boy suddenly appeared in front of me with the saddest face I have ever seen. I instantly knew he was the "Michael" of whom I had been foretold. His sorrow-ful eyes asked the question, "Why don't you want me?" Words were unnecessary to convey the message he came to deliver. I knew he was meant to be ours. He radiated such tremendous love that I reached to embrace him, at which point he backed up and disappeared right before my eyes.

Be assured, I never completed the phone call to schedule surgery. I could hardly wait to tell my husband of the visitation from our future son. That evening his heart was touched by my description. He had always wanted a son . . . but he was still reluctant to risk my life to another pregnancy. I at last fell asleep with the picture of my husband's troubled face in my mind. I knew he wanted God's will as much as I. I knew we would never knowingly deny a child the right to life, nor the right to join our family. And yet, the risks were great. I asked my husband to pray about our di-lemma. He initially refused, saying he knew what the answer would be and he could not bring himself to risk losing me.

But Michael wasn't about to give up on his reluctant future father. Apparently the time for Michael to come was getting close, and he really kept the pressure on.

After a restless night, my husband left for work early the next morning. I was preparing to go to the bookstore. My three-year-old daughter, Heather, was playing in the bedroom, and little Karen was in the front room with me.

Suddenly Heather shouted to her sister, "Karen, come quick and play with Michael."

Karen ran to the back of the house. I followed her immediately for three reasons: One, I knew for a fact there was nobody in the house but myself and the pre-school girls; two, the girls knew no one by the name of Michael at that time; three, I was lured by that name I had come to revere, *Michael.*

As I reached the bedroom, Heather said to Karen, "You're too late, he's gone."

I asked Heather, "Where did Michael go?"

"Right through there," she responded, pointing to a solid outside wall. She was very excited and showed no signs of fear whatsoever.

Again I told my husband the highlight of the day's events when he returned home. After hearing how Heather had seen "Michael," his faith was somewhat strengthened, yet he still had doubts as we fell asleep that night. It was he who related the next part of the story to me. You see, I am a fairly light sleeper when it comes to my children crying in the night. For some reason, that night I slept right through what my husband reported the next morning.

During the night, little Karen, who had run to see "Michael" the day before and missed seeing him, awakened fussing. When I did not respond, my husband arose to care for her. When asked what was the matter, Karen kept saying something beginning with the letter *b*. My husband finally guessed she was saying "bug" and assumed she'd had a nightmare. He held her and comforted her until she finally fell back to sleep. As he described this event in the morning, Karen became excited and again tried to explain what had awakened her. She repeated the strange *b* word from the night before. As I listened carefully, with that extra sense mothers have to understand their children, I recognized she was not saying "bug" but "boy."

"You saw a boy last night?" I asked in wonderment.

Karen nodded enthusiastically, happy to be correctly understood.

I continued, "Where did you see the boy?"

Karen ran down the hall and pointed to the ceiling of her room. By now our entire family was present.

Next I questioned, "What happened to the boy?"

Karen pointed up and replied, "Didn't hop, didn't skip, didn't jump."

Her gestures indicated the boy floated up from the

foot of her bed and out through the ceiling, departing the same way he had entered.

Cautiously my husband then queried, "Did he say his name?"

We all paused. . . .

"Michael."

"I give up!" exclaimed my husband as, palm pressed to forehead, he collapsed onto Karen's bed and gazed up toward heaven.

It was amazing! "Michael" had appeared three times in three days to three separate family members, two of whom were too young to fabricate such goings-on.

Shortly after my husband's surrender to faith, a fourth confirmation was provided. His father reported that "Michael" appeared to him in a dream, indicating he was indeed to join our family and that he had a special mission on earth.

Interestingly, after my husband accepted our son-to-be, my health began to improve. I conceived Michael within a few months, after having tried previously for three years. Again I had to be very careful and procure much bed rest because my condition was fragile.

We were able to sell the bookstore so I could stay home, reducing the threat of miscarriage. Miraculously, after several years of lengthy commutes, my husband was blessed with a better job close to home, so he was available on short notice when I needed help. I didn't have the strength to do much of anything. Neighbors, friends, and family kindly pitched in, enabling me to rest as frequently as needed to ensure that our last miracle baby would join our family.

When delivery day arrived, Michael entered the world via C-section. Our doctor had been through this with me before. He knew our chances of having a boy were medically very slim, but he also respected our heartfelt faith that this child would be a boy named Michael. There was a wonderful spirit of divine love in the delivery room as the infant came forth. The birth was such a remarkably touching moment that even the doctor shed tears of joy and gratitude with us as he delivered *a red-haired baby boy.*

Shortly after Michael's arrival, my female problems resumed, my health regressed, and I underwent the long-postponed surgery. But this time there was no anxiety . . . instead I enjoyed inner peace through the comforting assurance that I had filled God's will in "bearing" all children assigned to our family. The surgery was successful, and God had since blessed me with the health needed to continue the second portion of my maternal mission, "rearing" our children.

I believe these precious family relationships begin before earth life and continue after earth life. My story illustrates how eager some children are to come to their assigned families. Due to the dangers I faced in childbearing, we probably would have had only one child if two of our five children had not manifested to us their intent to join our family. Our children's pre-birth appearances gave my husband and me the courage to keep trying. Through the miracles I have shared, I now feel our family is complete, for which I am deeply grateful.

I conclude my story with two additional thoughts.

First, Michael, who is a redheaded ten-year-old at the time of this writing, does not like to be called Mike. Remember, he was so eager to come to this earth—to join our family in spite of my difficulties bearing children—that he encouraged us by appearing and/or speaking to family members five times before his birth. On four of those visits through the veil, he announced his name was Michael. Today this determined young man is still very firm that his name is *Michael.*

Lastly, my husband no longer asks who is missing at the dinner table.

—JANETTE P.

I derive my being from Him who was preexistent, and I go again to that which is my own, whence I came forth.

—GOSPEL OF PHILIP 64:10–12

Anjel

LET'S TAKE LIFE EASY NOW," BARRY REMARKED AS WE received the first copies of our second book, *Models of Love*, from the printer. It had been quite a challenge to finish the book while both our children were small and being home-schooled. I nodded my approval as Barry further commented, "Surely we can slow down now and make life simple and uncomplicated." No more challenges for a while, I thought as I sat hugging our new book to my heart.

Then I remembered a prayer I had made over a year ago. I asked that I never stop growing.

Our family, Barry and I, Rami, age ten, and Mira, age four and a half, packed up our old camper and set off for the mountains. Never had we needed a vacation more. On the third day of our camping trip, I was sitting alone when I felt the distinct presence of someone beside me. I knew this sensation well, for the same experience had happened twice to me, shortly before we conceived both Rami and Mira. At first, I felt in awe of the greatness of this being beside me, whom I could not see with physical eyes but could feel within my heart. "Maybe this is a helper," I thought, and then the message came:

"I am your third child and am ready to be conceived."

It was the last thing I wanted to hear at this time in my life.

"No!" I stammered. "I don't want to get pregnant. I don't want anything different right now. I just want to rest."

I felt this being smiling at me, loving me fully and offering the gift of its presence in my life.

I reflected on how I have always loved children. When I was ten years old and babysitting young ones, I made up my young mind to devote my life to children. When adults would ask me what I wanted to "be" when I grew up, I would always answer in the same way: "I want to be a mother."

Once again I was drawn back to the presence beside me, "You can conceive me in three weeks. Your family is now ready for my presence in your lives."

"No!" harshly echoed through my being.

Where was that "no" coming from in me? For the first time in my life I was feeling strong resistance to having another child. My rational mind argued that we

were both forty years old, too old to be having more
children, though I knew that wasn't true.

Barry and I had felt long ago that our family was
complete and had gotten rid of all the baby things. I
felt this great being stretch out its hands in blessing
and in love, seemingly amused by my obvious struggle.

The next three weeks were extremely confusing. Each
morning I would sit in meditation and feel my crazy
mind resist. The more I resisted, the more divine love
I felt pour upon me.

Finally, when my mind had come up with perhaps a
hundred reasons why we should not have another child,
this message came into my heart: "Your risk to conceive
me is your risk to be healed. . . . Trust in the perfection
of God's plan."

Against all that my rational mind was telling me,
the voice within my heart grew stronger and steadier.
I knew I needed to take a big risk and listen to my
heart, the will of my God-Self, and ignore my resisting
mind. God's will for us was to conceive our third child.

Joyce wasn't the only one struggling with resistance
to having another child. Our family felt very complete
to me, too.

In my deepest listening, the word that kept coming
to me was "surrender." But surrender to what? I wasn't
feeling the "knocking on the door" that Joyce was. I
wasn't even feeling the desire to have another baby.

So how could I surrender to something I wasn't even experiencing?

The answer came one day in a quiet, loving moment alone with Joyce. It was my greatest risk, my greatest leap of faith, to surrender to the guidance coming through Joyce. I had to let go of the little-boy part of me stubbornly "wanting to do it myself," even the part of me that wanted to understand what was happening. I had to accept my unknowingness.

At last, I felt a wave of peace come upon me, that unmistakable feeling that tells me I'm on the right track. I realized I wasn't surrendering to Joyce in the sense of giving my power away, the archetypal struggle of all little boys with their mothers. Rather, I was surrendering to God's will, to a plan I wasn't comprehending at this, my current, stage of development.

It became clear to me that, given the experiences Joyce was having, we could only conceive a child if it was for our highest good. My risk was simply to trust the perfection and goodness of the universe, to trust God.

I shared these thoughts and feelings with Joyce. The peace was contagious. The missing ingredient for her had been me. Up to that moment it had seemed a one-sided struggle, a decision that was hers alone. Now we were together accepting the gift of God—in whatever form it might come. If a soul was to come into our lives in the form of a new baby, it was, of course, a gift. We would be given the highest way to serve God,

COMING FROM THE LIGHT

for that was our highest desire. Whatever happened would be just what we needed, as it has always been in our lives.

Three days later, Barry and I said good-bye to our sweet girls and to Grandma and Grandpa, and journeyed to England where we attended a five-day retreat at the White Eagle Lodge. It was during this time that we both saw the full glory of the soul that had chosen to come to us as our third child. We felt so honored to have been chosen as parents for this one. As we became immersed in pregnancy for the third time, gratitude filled our being. I realized that this child was coming in answer to the prayer I had been saying for over a year. This one was coming to take us a big step further along our path. This was a step we could only make with help. Through the presence of this one in our lives, we would both experience a deep healing.

The risk to conceive our third child was like a leap in faith that was already reaping rewards. My mind still occasionally doubted the wisdom of our action, yet my heart knew that we were right on track.

With the excitement came an unexplainable feeling that this child would teach us about death. Barry and I tried to push the feeling away, thinking it was probably just a fear. However, it came all the more strongly. I had an uneasy feeling this baby would never grow to be an adult. My fear told me to have an amniocentesis.

My heart told me to trust. I trusted and I waited. Then severe nausea set in.

The second, third, and fourth months of pregnancy were extremely difficult. I was nauseous every minute of the day, having to spend most of my time lying down. There were times when I felt so discouraged by physical symptoms that I wished I would just die. It was during these times that I tried to remind myself that a great prize—the presence of this great being—was certainly worth the price of these months of hardship. But the nausea was so severe that I couldn't really feel the soul of our baby. The knowledge that the light surely follows the darkness kept me living each new day of this difficult initiation.

By four and a half months of pregnancy, I began to feel alive again in my body. I felt as if I were being born again into a new life from a period of death. The light was so bright. The baby began to grow within me and touch me lightly with its movement. I walked with confidence and joy, so happy to be carrying our third child.

We found a midwife at about the fifth month of pregnancy at a house-blessing of mutual friends. There were many people present, and she was sitting on the grass when we approached her. We bent down and greeted her with a hug. After a few minutes of conversing, Joyce asked her if she would consider helping with the pregnancy and birth. She looked at Joyce, smiled, and said she would have to think about it. Just then, our attention was diverted by other friends approaching and more greetings.

The next day, our midwife-friend called. She first asked us if she seemed to have acted strangely at the house-blessing, because she wanted to apologize. When we assured her she didn't, she told us what had happened. She said that when Joyce asked her to be her midwife, a bright light appeared around Joyce and she heard the words, "Of course you will." She felt almost in a state of shock and barely managed to mutter the few words that she did. This had never happened to her before, and she felt deeply moved. She felt the presence of our baby reaching out to touch her, really to choose her. From then on, she felt this presence, this soul, blessing her life as well. She had no choice but to be our midwife

During her first appointment with Barry and me, the midwife could not hear the baby's heartbeat with her regular stethoscope. She felt we had no need to worry as the presence and spirit of the baby was so strong. Often it is hard to hear the heartbeat at that stage with a regular instrument. Arrangements were made to meet again after Christmas for another check with a more sensitive instrument.

I was confident and assured that the baby was fine. Each day I rose early to meditate and asked to feel our baby's presence. Each day this presence was there stronger and stronger, not only assuring me that it was very much alive within me, but also gently guiding and instructing me. These mornings with our sweet babe became so precious to me. I was receiving a deep, spiritual training.

Several days before Christmas, I was filled with the realization that our baby was female and that her name was Anjel. The name filled me like an affirmation. I felt bathed in her presence. Each morning I woke with a sense of ecstasy at the glory of her being. "Oh, Barry," my first words of the morning would be, "her very essence is so beautiful. We are so blessed." Barry would smile and share my joy.

But I knew he was also concerned that I hadn't really grown much bigger in a month. He was looking forward to the next visit with our midwife and finally hearing the heartbeat.

The day of our appointment came. My meditation and time with my sweet "angel" was very special. As expert hands felt my uterus, concern crossed her tender face. "Joyce, you haven't grown. I want you to have an ultrasound test to determine what is happening."

Barry made the appointment immediately, and off we went with the children. As we drove to the hospital, Barry explained to us that this test would let us see the baby's movement and possibly determine why she didn't seem to be growing this last month. As I waited in the office while Barry and the children went to register for me, I reached into my purse and pulled out a little package of "Angel Cards." Each of the fifty cards had a picture of an angel with a corresponding word. The card I chose was the angel of gratitude—reminding me to be grateful for all that I am given, knowing it is a gift from God.

Stretched out on the X-ray table, I gathered the children and Barry close as the technician began scanning the uterus. Sadness etched her face, and her professional manner faltered. In one of the most awful moments of my life, she announced, "Your baby is dead." Rami and I burst out crying. Then the radiologist repeated the test and called Barry outside. Little Mira looked pale and confused. Extreme grief filled my being, and I was all set to jump into a tunnel of darkness when Mira spoke, "Mama, I'll take a boy rather than no baby at all. Will that help?"

Her innocence and purity touched my heart, and I smiled. In that moment, I knew that I was to be grateful for my two healthy children, rather than mourning the little dead body inside.

Lying in bed that night, my body ached from crying. I lay in a state of sadness. Unable to bear the sound of Barry sleeping, I woke him and said, "I need some wise words." He sat up in bed, rubbed his eyes, and tried to wake up. He gently rubbed my back and tenderly smiled.

"Why was I given so much assurance that the baby was alive?" I asked. "Is my intuition all wrong?" I needed the answers to these questions.

"Your intuition could never have been more right. Anjel has always been alive within you. You were connected to the vastness of her being and presence, far more than to the physical body in your womb. That's why you have looked and felt radiantly pregnant, even though the little body was not alive. Anjel never needed to be born in a physical way. Her greatest need was to give her love to the world through us. This she has been doing all along, and this pregnancy has deepened her link to us. The creation of a physical body had anchored her consciousness within us both. It has been a tremendous leap for all of us. Anjel has been born within us. We now have three children, two with physical bodies and one with a body of light. We have just as great a responsibility with our third child as with the other two. We are parents to Anjel in the sense that we are caretakers for a more evolved consciousness. We have the joyful responsibility of maintaining our connection with her. The work she will be doing requires that connection. In addition, we are like children and she our mother. We now know a spirit guide, a being who is holding us in her loving embrace while she works through us."

The next day, December 30, 1986, we went to have the D&E (dilation and evacuation, a procedure for removal of the dead fetus). Our obstetrician advised general anesthesia, and inwardly, we got the go-ahead. We prayed together for Joyce's protection and for the doctor's hands to be blessed and used as instruments of healing. Then Joyce was led away.

After an eternity, I opened my eyes to see our obstetrician beckoning me into a little room. Joyce was not awake yet from the anesthesia, but he wanted me to know all was well. He told me the little body was female, and then asked if I wanted to see it. I did, and followed him into another room. He went over to a counter, took the lid off a container and reached gently inside. Before taking the body out, he turned to me and warned me that it wouldn't be the prettiest sight.

I was prepared to see a fetus somewhat shrunken and macerated from lifelessness in the womb. But I was not prepared to see a face that reflected the timeless wisdom of the ages, a face that was in every way ancient, yet so completely devoid of life, just like an empty shell. I stood there looking at this face and body, holding it in my hands, and more deeply understanding the mystery of birth and death.

After much healing, I felt aglow again, the same sensation I had felt when holding Rami and Mira for the first time. Rather than being able to touch her with my hands, she gave me the gift of using these hands to touch others in blessing and love. Whenever I wanted to cradle her in my arms, all I needed to do was reach out and cradle another of God's precious children. Whenever I wanted to speak to her, all I had to do was to use my voice to give the gift of love to others.

Whenever I wanted to receive her inspiration, I only needed to sit in silence and ask.

She was born in the very heart of my being. She touched me physically with her small body so that we would always trust in her presence, like Jesus and his disciple Thomas. Through a constant receptivity to her, we are being set free.

—JOYCE AND BARRY VISSELL[4]

For all souls are prepared to eternity, before the foundation of the world.

—SECOND ENOCH

⇒✕⇐

My Name Is James

MY EXPERIENCE WITH THE UNBORN IS VERY SIMPLE. WE had five children, plus one miscarriage, and were trying, at this point, not to have another baby. But in quiet moments, I would hear a small, almost audible voice say, "My name is James, and I'm ready to be born." This happened a few times, so I shared it with my husband.

I was a little excited, but my last baby was only two, and I was still thinking I was not ready to have another child. In addition, we were planning to leave for India to work as missionaries.

On my birthday, April 5, my husband took me out for dinner and afterward we were intimate. But I had no inkling that I was pregnant until we were on the plane heading for India, April 17. It was quiet, and I was praying. I felt the Lord speak to my heart, "Blessed is the fruit of the womb." I knew then that I was pregnant. Nine months later, James was born in Pune, India.

—Detrah H.

The soul originated in the heights. From another race am I, for the Father of Truth remembered me.

—ODES OF SOLOMON

⫯

I Have Your Name on Me

Wᴇ ʜᴀᴅ ᴛʀɪᴇᴅ ꜰᴏʀ ᴛᴇɴ ʏᴇᴀʀs ᴛᴏ ʜᴀᴠᴇ ᴄʜɪʟᴅʀᴇɴ ʙᴜᴛ were not successful. We became discouraged as the realization settled heavily on us that we would probably never have children. After discussing this with some good friends, they suggested we consider adoption.

One night shortly after this, I was having a nightmare. Suddenly in my dream there was a light and a peaceful feeling. In the light I saw a beautiful baby with big dark eyes. Peace came over me. He said, "I have been waiting a long time, and I have your name on me." He spoke these words as one adult speaks to another, but I saw a baby's face. I did not know if the baby was a boy or girl.

Shortly, we made plans to adopt a child. It seemed to be the right thing to do, and we were excited. Within a year, we finally received our phone call. The baby we were to adopt was born.

We had to wait seventy-two hours before we could pick up our son, Tyler. Two days after his birth, we were told the birth mother wanted to see him. This was not a good sign. In about ninety percent of those cases, the mother keeps the baby. I sat in my office praying. Suddenly I felt the presence of my stepfather, who had passed away many years previously. He assured me that all was well. I realized that it was the anniversary of my stepfather's death.

The adoption went fine—without complications. In fact, we were later told that when the birth mother held Tyler, she had the distinct impression come to her mind that it really was God's will that Tyler be raised by the adoptive family. We were grateful.

Three years later my sister had an experience in which my stepfather (her father) appeared to her in a dream. He told her: "Tyler is a great spirit and was my good friend in the spirit world. When he found out his birth mother wanted to give him up for adoption, I asked him if he would come to our family. Tyler agreed."

—DOROTHY AND JERRY N.

≫≪

I Met My Son on the Other Side

My JOURNEY BEGAN ON OCTOBER 9, 1985. MY HUS-
band, Terry, and I had taken a trip to Salt Lake City
in a final effort to save our crumbling marriage. That
day, having sadly concluded that we had no future
together, we prepared to fly our single-engine plane
home to California and file for divorce. Despite
strong and disturbing premonitions of danger, I
shrugged off my fears and boarded the plane. The
small craft flew into a snowstorm, and after a heart-
stopping ride, Terry managed to make an emergency
landing in Delta, Utah, about one hundred miles
from Salt Lake City. Convinced that we had been
saved by a miracle, I refused to get into the plane
again. I insisted on finishing the trip by car. When
Terry learned there were no car rentals available in
the small town, he convinced me to fly again, point-

ing out that the weather had cleared and it was only a fifteen-minute flight to the next town where we could rent a car. Reluctantly, I agreed.

Again ignoring my overwhelming feelings of doom, I entered the plane . . . and flew into a nightmare. No sooner were we airborne, than the tempest resumed. We found ourselves in a terrifying flight, battling disorienting weather with zero visibility. Abruptly our small aircraft slammed into the side of a mountain, exploding into a raging inferno. Terry emerged relatively unscathed, but I suffered severe, disfiguring burns over three-fourths of my body.

To avoid freezing to death, we began a tortuous four-hour descent in blinding fog down the icy mountain, over slashing barbed-wire fences and through snow-covered fields that led us to a highway, where we were finally picked up. We discovered we had been divinely guided in our journey down the mountain, for we had amazingly walked a straight path from the plane crash site to the highway. Later, Search and Rescue concluded, by following my bloody footprints back to the site, that if we had veered in any other direction we would have perished in the wilderness.

Upon our rescue from the side of the road, we were taken to a small hospital, where we were told that our condition was too critical to be treated in their facility. It was suggested that we be placed in an airplane and flown to the Salt Lake City Burn Unit for treatment.

I screamed in hysterical protest. There was no way that I was going to get back into another plane.

We were moved to an ambulance and began the trip to Salt Lake City. Shortly thereafter my breathing became labored. My head was swollen out beyond my shoulders. The pain of the burns was more than I could bear. Each breath was more painful than the last. I began to choke and gasp for air. A nurse bent down to my ear and whispered, "Stop trying. We will do all the work for you." Whereupon they tried to insert a breathing tube in my throat. Misunderstanding the statement "stop trying," my struggle for life ended. At that moment my spirit passed from this life to the next.

Abruptly my pain ceased. A journey through a long tunnel took my spirit to the other side, where I was met by my grandmother, who had passed on a year or two previously. Gently she shared with me the divinity of God and His desire that we live in the light of His love. She showed me the importance of being a mother and the value of things we do for our children. I saw that my sacrifices for my children had not been in vain. Although I had considered myself an unsuccessful mother, in reality I had helped my children more than I had realized.

Grandma waved her arm, and the ground opened before us. I looked and saw a severely burned woman lying on a hospital bed surrounded by doctors and nurses. Her face was bandaged.

"You will never be the same, RaNelle," Grandma said. "Your face will be altered and your body filled with pain. When you go back, you will have years of rehabilitation."

The words "when you go back" cut me like a knife. I didn't want to go back. But Grandma pointed out to me that my children needed me and that I had many additional things to accomplish in my life.

"No. I'm not going back to my body," I insisted.

In response, my grandmother swept open her arms and commanded, "Look!"

A rift opened in the space before us, and I saw a young man walking toward us. At first he seemed not to understand why he was there. Then he recognized me and looked stunned.

"Why are *you* here?" he asked in disbelief. His disbelief quickly turned to sadness, and he began weeping.

"What is the matter?" I asked. "Why are you crying?" I put my arms around him and tried to comfort him.

"Why are you here?" he repeated.

Suddenly I understood. It was my refusal to return to earth that was causing his grief. I belonged on earth *to mother him.* I immediately felt guilt for my selfishness.

His name was Nathaniel. He had not yet been born on earth. He said that if I didn't go back, his *own* mission would be hindered. Then he showed me his mission. I saw that I was to open doors for him, to help him, to encourage him.

I realized that if I refused to return to my body on earth, I would be hurting him and everyone that he was to help in his mission.

"Oh, Nathaniel," I said. "I swear to you that I will help you. I promise that I will go back and do everything that I can to do my part. I will open doors for you. I will protect and encourage you. I will give you everything that I have. Nathaniel, you *will* complete your mission. I love you."

His grief was replaced with gratitude. His face lit up, and I saw the great spirit that he is. He was crying again, but this time with appreciation and joy.

"Thank you," he said. "Oh, I love you, Mom."

My spirit was thrilled, but I was unable to respond to him because things began happening very quickly. I was moving again.

"RaNelle," Grandmother said. "There is one more thing I need to say to you. Tell everyone the key is love."

"The key is love."

"The key is love," she repeated.

Then she let go of my hand. The word *love* reverberated in my mind as I left her and fell into a deep blackness. I was crying as I left the world of light and glory and love.

The last thing I saw on the other side was Grandmother's outstretched hand.

The love I felt from heaven sustained me through the painful days and months that followed my return to my body. My sufferings over the next year and a half shifted from my skin and tissues and settled in my inner organs. The stress of the burns had caused my body to begin shutting down internally. My physician felt that I should have a hysterectomy soon. If I delayed, he warned, the operation would become mandatory rather than optional. I wanted two other opinions, but realized that the only expert I needed was myself. I had seen Nathaniel and knew that his destination was this earth.

I made eating and lifestyle changes. About a month and a half later a miracle occurred. I told my OBGYN that I needed a pregnancy test. "Are you aware of the term 'hysterical pregnancy'?" he asked skeptically. "Let's wait for a month or two to see if your 'pregnancy' symptoms persist."

Eight months later I went into labor and gave birth to a wonderful healthy baby *girl!* This wasn't what I had expected! Of course I loved my daughter dearly, but what of Nathaniel?

As the years went by, discussions of divorce surfaced again. On "the other side" choices were so clear they were obvious, but here in the world things become clouded and unsure. Was I really to bear Nathaniel?

Would he come into this life to a troubled marriage? Again I became pregnant, but the questions haunted me. I couldn't see how Nathaniel could come into a situation like this. He would need the stability of a strong family because so much depended upon his life's mission.

In spite of my concerns, I reached term and the contractions finally turned into the birth process. The hauntingly beautiful melody of *"Somewhere In Time"* was playing on a stereo near my bed. An impression came to me that I was being watched from my right side. I turned and saw a man standing there, a tall man with dark hair and blue eyes. He was dressed in a white suit. His eyes were wide and mournful. I had seen those eyes before, those sorrowful eyes. But now he was lamenting the pain I was going through, the suffering I was experiencing for him. He opened his mouth and said, "Thank you, Mom," and a wave of love came into me that blew my spirit into a spin. I looked at him through tears and said, "Thank you." Then he was gone. And my heart was filled.

I gave a final push and heard a little cry. My coach, Annie, said, "You've got a beautiful baby boy, RaNelle. I hope you've got a name for him."

Terry came forward and looked at the baby, and Annie let him clip the cord. "It's Nathaniel, isn't it?" he said.

I nodded, still crying.

"Thank you, Nathaniel, thank you for bringing our family together again. Thank you for giving me the strength and courage to carry on, to clearly understand my mission and role as a mother.

Now it is your turn. . . ."

—from *The Burning Within* by RaNalle Wallace with Curtis Taylor, Gold Leaf Press, 1995[5]

Author Notes:
Our Eternal Spirit

I LOVE OLD MOVIES. ONE OF MY FAVORITES IS *The Blue Bird*, taken from the classic play by Maeterlinck, a Belgian dramatist and Nobel Prize winner. In this film, there is a beautiful scene depicting children leaving the celestial realms of heaven and coming to earth. The children know that earth life is a great part of their opportunity to grow and develop as children of God. As part of their development, they need mortal bodies to house their eternal spirits. As they tearfully bid good-bye to their friends in heaven, they know that the memory of their pre-earth life will be veiled in forgetfulness. They understand that some of them will have long life spans, and others mere moments of time, but their individual missions are clear. They prepare to come down.

As one group approaches the earth, the voices of the children are heard to cry: "The earth! The earth! I can see it; how beautiful it is! How bright it is!"

Following their cries of ecstasy comes a sweet song of gentleness and expectancy from the earth below. Maeterlinck explains: "It is the song of the mothers coming out to meet them."

Although Maeterlinck's play concerning the origin of man is philosophical in nature, there is considerable historical, evidence to substantiate his theory. In the New Testament, Christ spoke frequently about our premortal life. For example, He prayed to the Father, "Glorify thou me with thine own self with the glory which I had with thee before the world was" (John 17:5). Jesus also referred to this belief when he declared, "My kingdom is not of this world" since it originated "out of the world" "before the world was" (John 18:36, 17:6,5).

A belief in a preexistence was also the premise upon which the disciples based their question about the blind man: "Master, who did sin, this man or his parents, that he was born blind?" (John 9:2). In fact, so realistic was their conception of a preexistence that contemporary Jews described the very chambers (Hebrew *gut, aroboth*) in which these souls dwelled awaiting their turn to descend into bodies. The *Genesis Rabbah* even tells how God took counsel with such spirits before creating the world. The Old Testament confirms this notion, when the Lord, in a description of a glorious premortal day, asked Job, "Where wast thou when I laid the foundations of the earth . . . and all the sons of God shouted for joy?" (Job 38:4,7)

Early Christianity likewise continued to tell how the "chambers of souls" longed to deliver the spirits "entrusted to them from the beginning," just as the womb longs to "complete its anguish of labor" (4 Ezra 4:33–43; cf. Rev. 6:9–11). Such writings also indicate that a definite number of souls exist (cf. Deut. 32:8, Acts 17:26) and that the coming of the Messiah will be delayed until all have had their chance to come to earth (4 Ezra 4:35–36; 2 Baruch 23:3–5; 2 Enoch 23:4–5; 49:2, Pistis Sophia 22).

To prophets, and even to mothers and fathers, throughout the Bible, the coming of unborn children was foretold. The angel Gabriel revealed to Zacharias that his wife, Elizabeth, would have a son in her old age (Luke 1:13–19). When Elizabeth was six months pregnant with John the Baptist, the angel Gabriel also came to the Virgin Mary, telling her that she, too, would have a son, the son of the Highest, and she should call his name Jesus (Luke 1:30–32).

Over eight hundred references to the pre-earth existence of mankind have been identified in Jewish and Christian sources from the time of Christ until the sixth century A.D. Early Hellenistic (Greek) writings also referred to belief in a pre-earth life. However, after the sixth century A.D., mention of a life before mortality virtually disappears from orthodox Jewish, Christian, and Greek writings (Hamerton-Kelley, R.G., *Pre-Existence, Wisdom and the Son of Man in the New Testament*, Cambridge University Press, 1973).

A premortal existence was discussed by such well-known ancient philosophers as Plato, and Christian writers Origen of Alexandria and Justin Martyr. The writings of the ancient Jewish historian Josephus and the Jewish theologian Philo (who claimed that everything he wrote agreed with the Pentateuch) show that belief in a premortal life was evident in Judaism until the 5th century A.D., which in certain quarters held that the soul longs to return to that premortal existence after earth life (*Judische Theologie*, 212–228).

The doctrine of a premortal existence was condemned by the council of Constantinople in A.D. 553 However, *Hastings Encyclopedia of Religion and Ethics* reports the doctrine of a pre-existence was favored by Origen (the greatest of early church theologians), Justin Martyr, Augustine, Cyril of Jerusalem, Pierius, John of Jerusalem, Rufinius, Nemesius, and the Western Church generally until the time of Gregory the Great (article on pre-existence, p. 239).

More recently, Dr. Wayne Dyer, referring to the research of Sir Aldous Huxley, said:

Aldous Huxley in *The Perennial Philosophy* studied every age and every civilization and found there were three factors that were a part of every human age and every civilization that ever existed. These were civilizations that never had any contact with each other at all; primitive tribes, Buddhists, eastern philosophies, cave men, etc.; they all believed three things:

1. There is an infinite world beyond the world of the changing; there is some kind of an existence that is in back of this physical world that we find ourselves in and that we are awake in.

2. The second thing they all believed is that an infinite world is a part of every human personality . . . that it is a part of every human being.

3. And the third thing they have all believed and that is a part of every culture is that the purpose of life and of being here is to discover God or to discover that invisible world which we call God.

The life before is spoken of in the legends of Africa, in the traditions of Native Americans, and in the myths of other cultures. An excerpt from Alex Haley's book *Roots* serves as an example:

He said that three groups of people lived in every village. First were those you could see—walking around, eating, sleeping, and working. Second were the ancestors whom Grandma Yaisa had now joined.

"And the third people—who are they?" asked Kunta.

"The third people," said Omoro, "are those waiting to be born."

—HALEY, ALEX, *Roots*.
New York: Doubleday, 1976, p. 29.

Ancient writings, such as the *Dead Sea Scrolls* and the *Nag Hammadi Texts,* also make specific mention of a life before earth life. The *Dead Sea Scrolls* were discovered in Qumran, in the current state of Israel, in 1947. The *Nag Hammadi Texts* were discovered in upper Egypt in 1946. The *Book of Thomas,* from the *Nag Hammadi Texts,* is widely recognized by Christian scholars as a collection of sayings by Jesus. Many believe they were recorded as Christ taught the people, often just a select few, during the forty days after the Resurrection.

These ancient texts have only within recent years been translated and made available to the general public. They are full of quotations and comments about the origin of man.

According to the *Book of Thomas,* it is the secret knowledge of one's true nature that assures immortality. Jesus said, in these ancient texts, "If they say to you, from where have you originated? say to them, we have come from the Light, where the Light has originated through itself. If they say to you, who are you? say, we are His sons and we are the elect of the Living Father" (Logion 50).

Poets, too, have sung the words of immortality and have been so inspired by the belief in a life before as to leave us with great verses of meditation. From Wordsworth's "Ode on Intimations of Immortality":

> Our birth is but a sleep and a forgetting:
> The Soul that rises with us, our life's Star,
> Hath had elsewhere its setting,
> And cometh from afar:
> Not in entire forgetfulness,
> And not in utter nakedness,
> But trailing clouds of glory do we come
> From God, who is our home:
> Heaven lies about us in our infancy!

Today, we are living in a world that is increasingly open to spiritual ideas. In the last twenty years, the scientific study and acceptance of the near-death experience (NDE), in particular, once thought to be a mystical, even delusional experience, has gained validity as a scientific phenomenon, thanks to the works of Dr. Elisabeth Kübler-Ross in the 1970s and the landmark publication of Dr. Raymond Moody's best-seller, *Life After Life,* in 1975.

Near-death research has led to the discovery of additional transcendental or spiritually transforming experiences that have similar elements to the NDE, but do not require a near-death encounter to be elicited. In 1984, Dr. Kenneth Ring reported that there were accounts of over one hundred spiritually transforming non-NDEs in the International Association for Near-Death Studies (IANDS) files.

Coming from the Light adds to the growing body of literature that is expanding our concept of existence. While the NDE explores where we go after life, this book explores the phenomena of prebirth experience (PBE) and considers where we lived before this life. Like the NDE, the PBE and other transcendental experiences seem to not only be increasing, but increasingly reported. It is as though mankind is undergoing a spiritual renaissance to counterbalance the increase in chaos and despair in the world.

Some scientists have expressed concern that the scientific revolution has dominated the world with its insistence on objectivity, reliability, and validity. This approach to truth has accomplished much, including the eradication of deadly diseases and placing men on the moon. However, strict scientific methods have also limited the quest for truth by denying aspects of experience that cannot be readily observed or measured. As Dr. Melvin Morse has suggested, the human soul will never be found in the scientific laboratory.

The prebirth experience and the near-death experience provide a unique perspective on the value of life, the purpose of life, and accountability for life. Near-death experiencers report a sense of "returning home" when their spirit temporarily crosses to the other side. One cannot "return to" if one has not "come from." What is this place we "return to"? The PBE provides evidence that we "come from" the same place we "return to." It has been called our heavenly home, our eternal home, the source of our origin. In other words, we come from the Light and return to the Light.

You come from a premortal life with a special mission to perform. You are here now by special appointment. This is your time in the whole history of the earth, the time that you were appointed to receive a mortal body and fill your purpose. You are here on an errand from God. You can do much good. Serving your fellow man is a key to filling your mission . . . in your home, your job, your neighborhood, or your world. Whether your influence is large or small on earth, the goal is that it be positive and loving. By learning and then fulfilling your mission on the earth, you can experience peace and joy. What power there is in knowing that you are not an accident, that you are eternal! When you discover that you are an eternal spirit, that you lived in a heavenly realm before your mortal birth and you will return to a heavenly realm at death—then you will discover the essence of your divine nature. In his book *The Seven Spiritual Laws of Success*, Deepak Chopra has stated: "We must find out for ourself that inside us is a god or goddess in embryo that wants to be born so that we can express our divinity."

OUR ETERNAL SPIRIT

Listen to the whisperings of your inner spirit-self. Before birth, you were a royal child in the kingdom of heaven. There is a royal child within each soul, sometimes astray or misguided by earth trials, but the royal self is here for a purpose: to overcome, to fill a mission, to return Home in glory.

Your royal destiny is found in His title—King of kings.

Discover the royal child within. . . .

—SARAH HINZE
Mesa, Arizona
April, 1996

Afterword

A Comparison of the NDE and the PBE (the near-death experience and the prebirth experience)

by Brent Hinze, Ph.D.

(dedicated to Sarah, for our 25th wedding anniversary)

Life before Life and *Life after Life*

One evening a few years ago, after the nightly marathon of getting our nine children bedded down for the night, Sarah and I surprisingly discovered we had survived the day with sufficient energy to discuss her ideas for a book on life *before* life. As we spoke in rare privacy, we had an "aha insight." We envisioned an additional dimension to the spectrum identified by Dr. Raymond Moody's 1975 best-seller, *Life After Life*. His book described a phenomenon that had previously received little research attention—the near-death experience (NDE). Dr. Moody and other authors and researchers have made the NDE a household word. George Gallup, Jr., has estimated that more than eight million people have had NDEs in America (approximately one of every thirty people).

That evening, Sarah and I theorized there is evidence

for life before life, as well as life after life. We sketched the human life-stages spectrum as follows:

Life Stages Spectrum
Life before Life . . . Earth Life . . . Life after Life

Evidence for the "life before" comes from a spiritual experience similar to the NDE. For example, in an NDE the spirit-self temporarily leaves the physical body and crosses over to a realm beyond earth life. In a typical life-before-life or prebirth experience (PBE), a spirit not yet born into mortality crosses over from the pre-earth life and appears to or communicates with someone on earth. The preborn soul often announces they are ready to advance from their premortal existence by being born into earth life. Our research indicates that there is a continuity of self, that the "same you" progresses through each of the three life stages.

We knew that Sarah and a few friends had seen or heard from their preborn children through "announcing dreams" or spiritual encounters before they were conceived, and that some people experienced déjà vu or memories of their life before earth life. We speculated that the PBE occurs to many persons, as does the NDE. So Sarah began a quest to support her belief that each individual is unique, special, and begins their eternal journey long before earth life. In short, before you were born, the very essence of you, your spirit self, lived in a heavenly realm.

Quest to Verify the Prebirth Experience

Now, my father is a veterinarian and my uncle is a dog trainer. I grew up around animals. I have seen beautiful, well-trained hunting dogs in action. They will go over, under, around, or swim through obstacles to reach their objective. In that spirit, I affectionately came to refer to my wife, Sarah, as a "bird-dogger." I have been amazed as I firsthand watched this busy homemaker turn into a gentle but persistent bird-dogger.

In the five years or so since Sarah began her quest, she has contacted researchers of spiritual phenomena from around the world. She has studied book after book on near-death and related spiritual research. She has placed requests for prebirth case histories in newspapers in the United States and other countries. She has appeared on radio and television shows, written articles and spoken to live audiences about prebirth experiences and the evidence of our life before life. She joined the International Association for Near-Death Studies. She has pursued every lead on prebirth experiences like a skilled hunting dog. In short, she has become a true bird-dogger.

(For my part, I have typed and edited her manuscripts and worked extra hours to pay her phone bills!)

PBE Research, 20 Years behind NDE Research

Dr. Moody had documented about one hundred fifty NDE case studies when he published *Life after Life* in

1975. (He now estimates he has personally heard over 10,000 NDEs.) By 1995 Sarah had about one hundred fifty PBE case studies on file. This parallel to Dr. Moody's work suggests the research on prebirth experiences today is about where the near-death research was twenty years ago. By learning from the pioneering lessons of NDE research, PBE research will hopefully progress faster.

An Analysis of PBE Traits

As I became increasingly involved in Sarah's research, I "holed up" in my office throughout a four-day weekend and analyzed a sample of 33 PBE case studies she was considering for publication. When I emerged on the fourth day, I had a much better understanding of the nature of the PBE. Following editing decisions, 30 of the 33 original stories (91%) ended up in this book. Sarah asked me to share my findings in this afterword, as a gift for our twenty-fifth wedding anniversary. The cases reviewed document a variety of types of prebirth experiences. Since more than one PBE may occur to a person or family, the thirty-three original cases contained 57 PBEs, which included the following categories:

When PBEs Occur:

Before conception—In 53% of the PBEs studied the preborn being was witnessed before conception.

After conception, before birth—In 47% of the PBEs the preborn being was witnessed after conception, but before birth.

To whom PBEs occur:

Mothers—In 63% of the PBEs the preborn being was witnessed by the mother-to-be.

Fathers—In 13% of the PBEs the preborn being was witnessed by the father-to-be.

Parents—Thus in 76%, or about ³/₄ of the PBEs, the preborn being was witnessed by parents, natural or adoptive.

Others—In 24%, or nearly ¹/₄ of the PBEs, the preborn being was witnessed by siblings, grandparents, self in flashbacks, other relatives, close friends, and midwives.

Where PBEs Occur:

Forty-four of fifty-seven preborn beings were witnessed in America, the main area of our research thus far. PBEs were also obtained from Australia, England, Canada, the Navajo Indian Nation, and the Blackfoot Indian Nation. (One PBE took place in an airplane while flying over India, which I did not know where to assign. Perhaps an airline, "Air India," gets credit for that one.)

Hypothesis:

From our initial research, we hypothesize the PBE is universal, like the NDE, occurring in all races and cultures.

Types of PBEs:

Visions—29 preborn beings were witnessed in visions, appearances to the PBEr in a waking state.
Dreams—16 preborn beings were witnessed in dreams, appearances while the PBEr was asleep. (Some cultures call these experiences "announcing dreams.")
Hearing—20 preborn beings were witnessed by hearing a voice message from or about the preborn.
Telepathy—13 preborn beings were witnessed by communication directly to the PBEr's mind (telepathic or spiritual communication, as often described in NDEs).
Escort to Earth—29 PBEs indicated an escort who brought the preborn to earth.
Adoption—3 PBEs announced the child would be birthed by a biological parent, but was to be adopted by the parent(s) who witnessed the PBE.
Déjà vu, memories, flashbacks—8 individuals recalled (or still recall) aspects of their life before earth life.

Former-life language—2 individuals recalled speaking another language in the life before.
The light—10 individuals reported seeing a brilliant light in the PBE, similar to the light seen in many NDEs.

Comparison of a "Typical" NDE and PBE

Researchers have identified characteristics that frequently occur in a "typical" NDE, such as the spirit-self leaving the body, going through a tunnel, feeling great love and peace, witnessing a brilliant light or being(s), etc. Depending on which list one reviews, there are up to fifteen typical events that have been described in NDEs. Not all occur in each NDE, but some combination of these characteristics is generally agreed to constitute a genuine NDE.

Similarly, a pattern of "typical" PBE traits is emerging. A prebirth experience contains some combination of the following:

Ten aspects of a "typical" prebirth experience:

Radiation of love—The preborn radiates a powerful love to the prebirth experiencer, similar to the love felt from the light in the NDE.
Celestial light—The preborn may radiate, or appear in, a brilliant light that does not hurt the eyes

and conveys extraordinary peace, similar to the light in the NDE.

Thankful and eager to come to earth—The preborn is excited about earth life, views it as a growth opportunity, and is thankful that the parents are providing this opportunity. Yet there may be some fear of the unknown in facing the transition to earth life.

Leaving a loving heavenly home—The preborn is eager to enter earth life, but expresses a degree of loss or apprehension at leaving the sanctuary of his heavenly home.

A time to come to earth—The preborn often indicates that the time in which one comes to earth is assigned, as part of a divine timetable, so personalized growth experiences can be achieved.

A unique mission—The preborn message conveys that each individual has special purposes or missions to accomplish during his specified time on earth.

Protection/Warning—Some preborn appearances provide protection or warning to the recipient. (In the case studies reviewed, aid to the PBErs was provided by the preborn to prevent or recover from suicide attempts, abuse, rape, birth control, and abortion that would block the preborn's conception and birth on earth.)

Messages—Some preborn appearances provide messages about something the future parent(s) or

others must do as part of their earth mission or
to help the preborn.

Escort to earth—Some preborn are brought to
earth by an escort (just as some NDErs are escorted to the life after life).

Déjà vu—Some PBEs consist of memories or
flashbacks of one's pre-earth life.

Additional Evidence for a Life Before

In addition to the personal accounts collected and
shared in Sarah's book, our research has identified other
references to the concept that we live and progress in
a life before earth life. These references come from
such varied sources as ancient and modern literature,
poetry, philosophy, religions, the Dead Sea Scrolls, the
Nag Hammadi Texts, the scriptures, other ancient writings, folklore and legends passed down from generation
to generation. Thus, belief in a life before is found in
many races and cultures. Some of this data can be
found in quotations interspersed throughout this book.
For our present purpose I quote a single reference:

> *And it shall come to pass afterward, that I will
> pour out my spirit upon all flesh; and your sons and
> your daughters shall prophesy, your old men shall
> dream dreams, your young men shall see visions:*
>
> *And also upon the servants and upon the hand-
> maids in those days will I pour out my spirit.*

*And I will shew wonders in the heavens and in
the earth. . . .*

— *Joel 2: 28–30*

Are We Experiencing a Spiritual Outpouring?

Why is so much spiritual information coming forth
at this time in history. For example, a review of today's
media identifies numerous books, articles, seminars,
movies, television programs, and so forth on near-death
experiences, angels, miracles, etc. The data suggest spiritual experiences are both increasing and increasingly
reported. This information challenges the theory that
humans exist only during their time on earth. Just a
few short years ago spiritual data was considered unsci-
entific and even delusional. Several centuries ago one
could have been burned at the stake for expressing such
beliefs. What has happened?

I feel present-day conditions have created a great
need to better understand the purpose of life.

We observe that in spite of major advances in science, medicine, the industrial revolution, the media
and information explosions, we are witnessing a sig-
nificant decline in social skills, mental health, and
personal safety in many parts of the world. It was
recently reported that there are over forty wars or
armed conflicts in various countries of the world. In
the Phoenix area, where we live, there was nearly a

murder per day in 1994 as a result of drive-by shootings, gang wars, rapes, kidnapping, bombings, robberies, etc. This type of trauma occurs all over America and the globe. And the trend is growing. This is not a picture of an enlightened or advanced world. In spite of our progressing knowledge of "things," people skills are regressing.

Interest in a higher existence was illustrated in the November 28, 1994, issue of *Newsweek,* "The Search for the Sacred: America's Quest for Spiritual Meaning," which confirmed that people are asking, "Why are we here? What is the purpose of our existence?" Furthermore, we see best-sellers in fiction and non-fiction about the spiritual nature of man, suggesting there is more to life than science alone can measure. Evidence is multiplying that there *is* a higher essence within each of us. We must tap into that higher essence before we destroy ourselves and Gaia (Mother Earth).

In *Heading Toward Omega,* Dr. Kenneth Ring reports his research-based belief that spiritual experiences *are* increasing in the world (including the NDE, the PBE, angels, miracles, etc.) and that many people are indeed moving toward a higher essence he calls Omega. A clue to higher growth is seen in the personality changes observed in many spiritual experiencers that eventually lead them to happier, more loving, more service-oriented, more fulfilling lives. In short, they are transformed.

Dr. Ring reports that one does not have to "nearly

die" to grow spiritually. We can learn from others: individuals who hear about, visualize, or read about NDEs and other spiritually transforming experiences (including, we hypothesize, PBEs) also become more loving, more service-oriented, more enlightened, and more fulfilled. Such individuals sense their divine origin and purpose in life, as well as that of their fellow beings. They have higher self-esteem and higher respect for others—keys to a higher life.

Contemplate the power in spiritually transforming experiences: if you were visited by your child before their birth, if you were shown your child is eternal and comes from the Light with a mission to perform on earth, would it not increase your love and awe in nurturing your child . . . and all children? Would not your own self-esteem and sense of purpose become precious by knowing of your divine origin and destiny? Does not respect for life increase by learning of our eternal nature through PBEs, NDEs, etc.? It is difficult to imagine such tragedies as abuse, rape, and murder taking place if both parties understand that we are eternal, that we probably knew each other before this life and will surely face each other again in a life review in the next life . . . in the presence of the Light!

My point is, we may not all have the opportunity to see through the veil, but we can learn from the experiences of those who do. We can use this spiritual knowledge about the sacred and eternal nature of life to raise our values to a higher level for ourselves, our families, and our world. A cosmic knowledge of the nature of the soul can eternally enhance our love of self and others.

Yes, it appears we are indeed in the midst of a spiritual outpouring.

Lastly, I share a meaningful experience. After lecturing on life before life in New York City we returned to our hotel room where Sarah related:

> A lady approached me after my part of our lecture. She described attending a seminar where Dr. Elisabeth Kübler-Ross told of a couple with a little girl and a newborn baby. The girl kept asking to be alone with the baby. The parents were concerned about her request because they had heard of sibling rivalry. The small child repeated her request for several days. Finally, the parents permitted her a solo visit with the baby, but they monitored the event by listening on the intercom to the newborn's room. The young girl entered the nursery. All was quiet for a moment. Then the parents heard the girl child whisper to her infant brother, "Tell me about God. I'm forgetting."
>
> Dr. Kübler-Ross concluded, "That, my friends, the spiritual origin of man—where we come from before birth—that is the next great area of research."
>
> The lady finished her story and hugged me, saying, "Sarah, I think you have begun . . ."

To Join the Search for the Royal Child Within:

If you or others you know have spiritual experiences or insights to share, or for information on lectures and seminars on "Discovering the Royal Child Within," please contact:

ROYAL CHILD STUDIES
Sarah and Brent Hinze
P.O. Box 31086
Mesa, AZ 85275-1086
602-898-3009

End Notes

1. Richard G. Ellsworth, "Growing Toward the Good," *The New Era*, Salt Lake City, Utah, May 1986, pp. 8–10. Used with permission.

2. Tracey Nelson, as told to Cassandra Eason, *A Mother's Instincts, The Extraordinary Intuitions of Ordinary Women*, Collins Publishers London, Aquarian Press: Harper 1992, p. 69.

3. Betty Clark Ruff, *Instructor*, "My Toddler Taught Me About Preexistence and Death," February 1963, p. 61.

4. Joyce and Barry Vissell, *Risk To Be Healed*, Ramira Publishing, CA, 1989, pp. 13–57.

5. RaNelle Wallace with Curtis Taylor, *The Burning Within*, Gold Leaf Press: Placerville CA, 1994.